BRODY'S GHOST ™

BOOK 1

STORY AND ART BY
MARK CRILLEY

DARK HORSE BOOKS®

THIS BOOK IS DEDICATED TO JILL THOMPSON,
WHO BELIEVED IN THIS SERIES
WHEN I'D ALMOST STOPPED
BELIEVING IN IT MYSELF.

Publisher - Mike Richardson
Designer - Tony Ong
Assistant Editor - Patrick Thorpe
Associate Editor - Katie Moody
Editor - Dave Land

Published by Dark Horse Books
A division of Dark Horse Comics, Inc.
10956 SE Main Street
Milwaukie, OR 97222

darkhorse.com

To find a comic shop in your area call the Comic Shop Locator Service toll-free at (888) 266-4226

First edition: July 2010
ISBN 978-1-59582-521-6

BRODY'S GHOST BOOK 1

10 9 8 7 6 5 4 3 2
Printed by Transcontinental Gagné, Louiseville, QC, Canada.

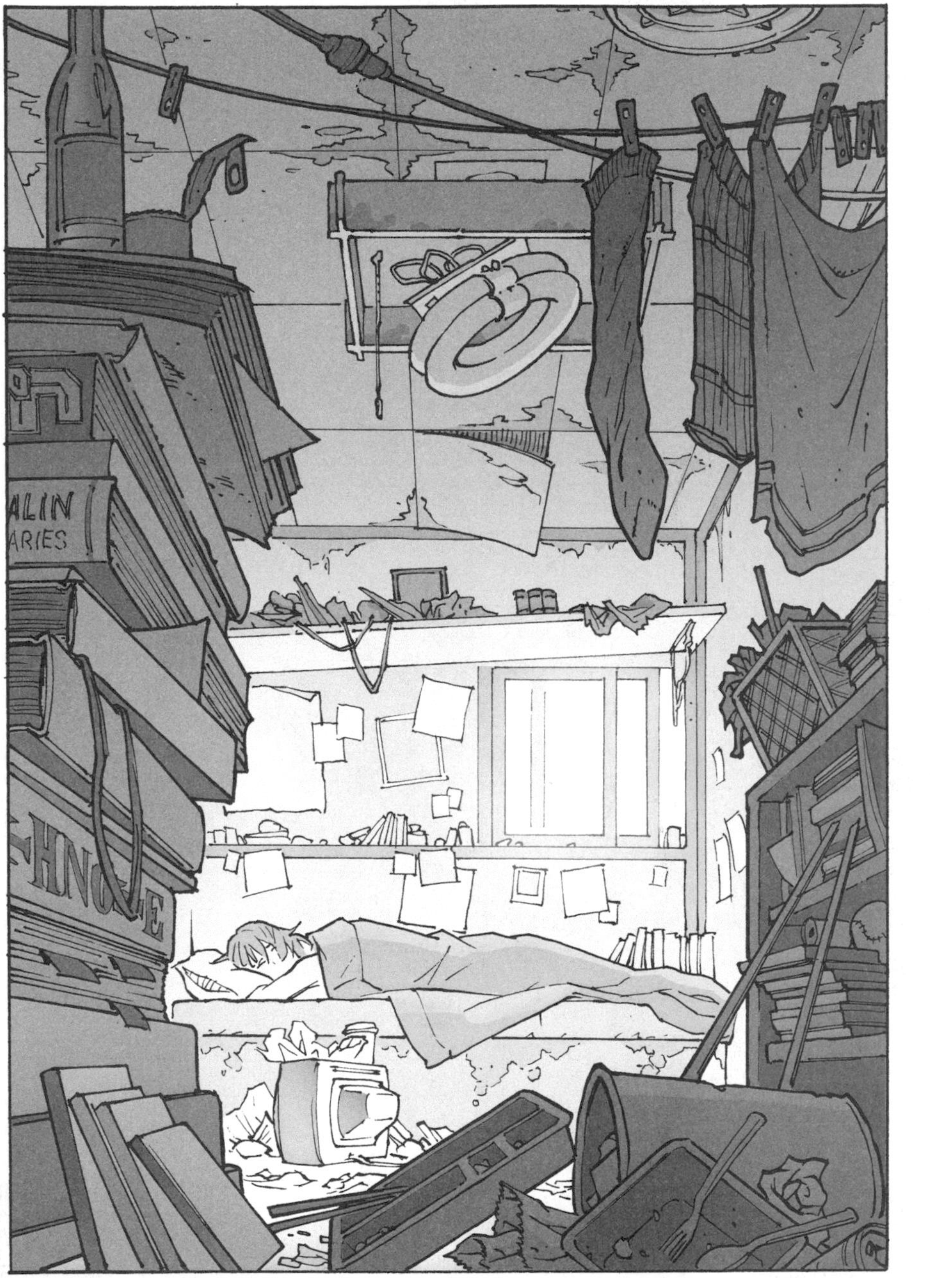
ALIN
ARIES

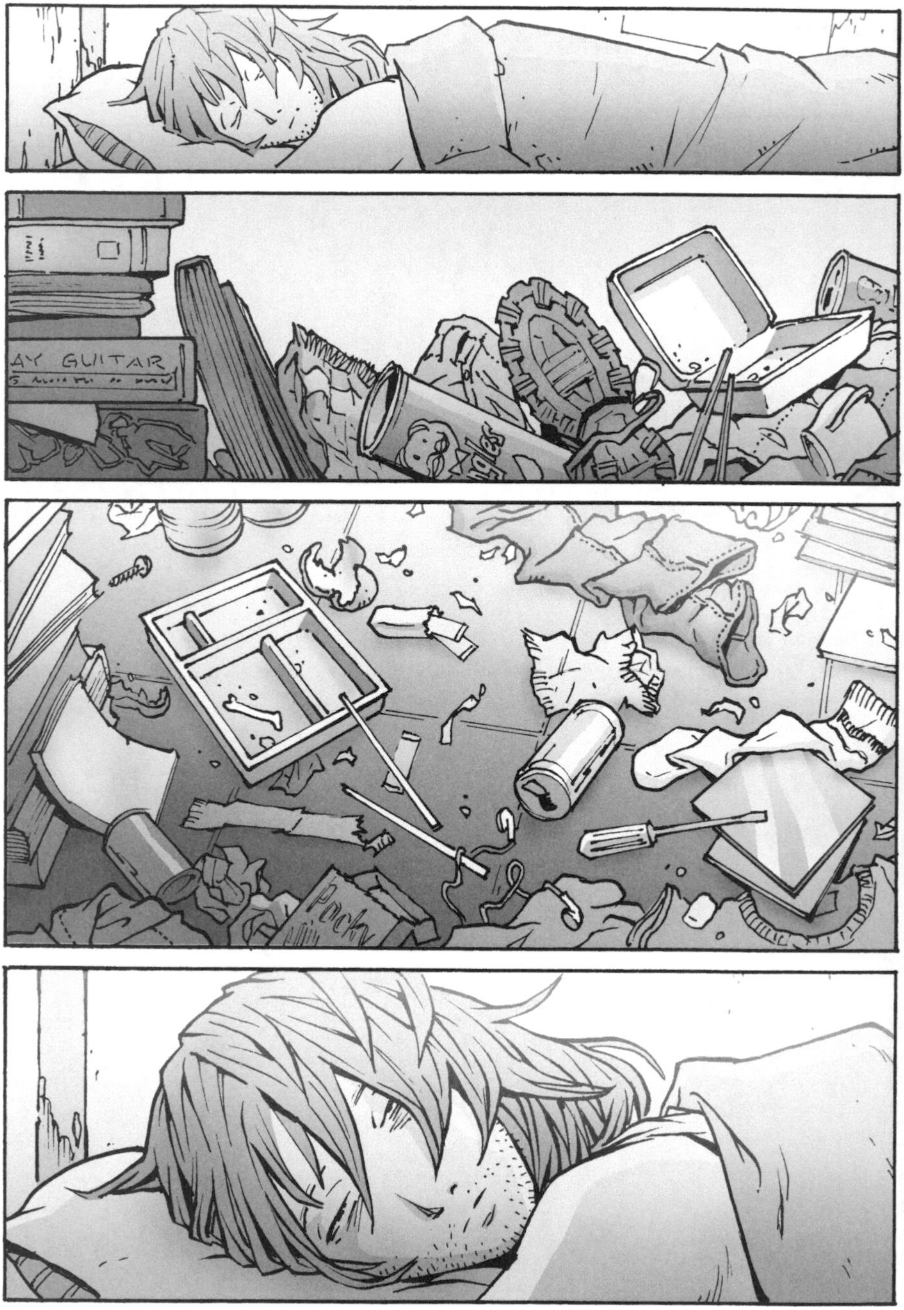
AY GUITAR

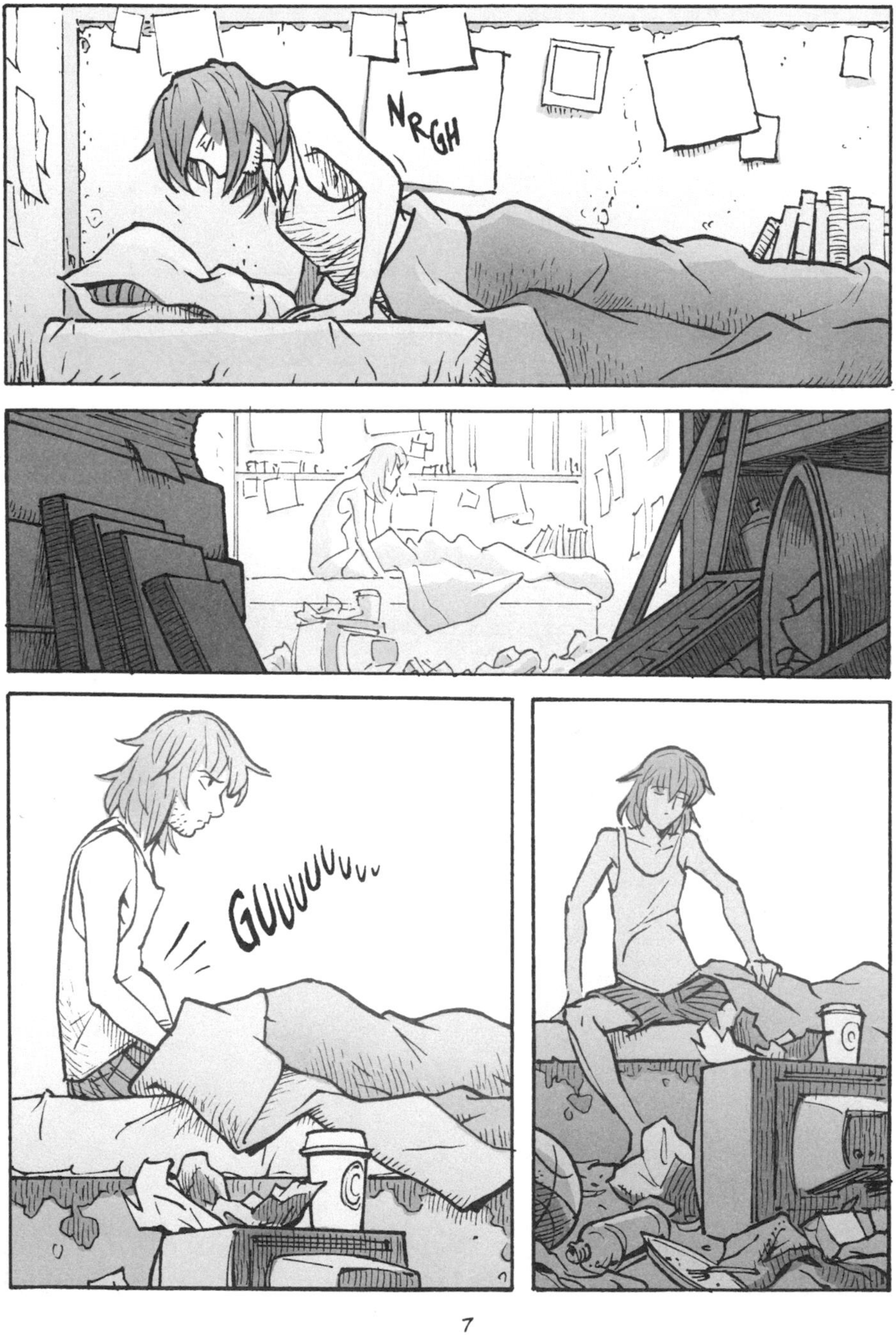
NRGH
GUUUUUUU

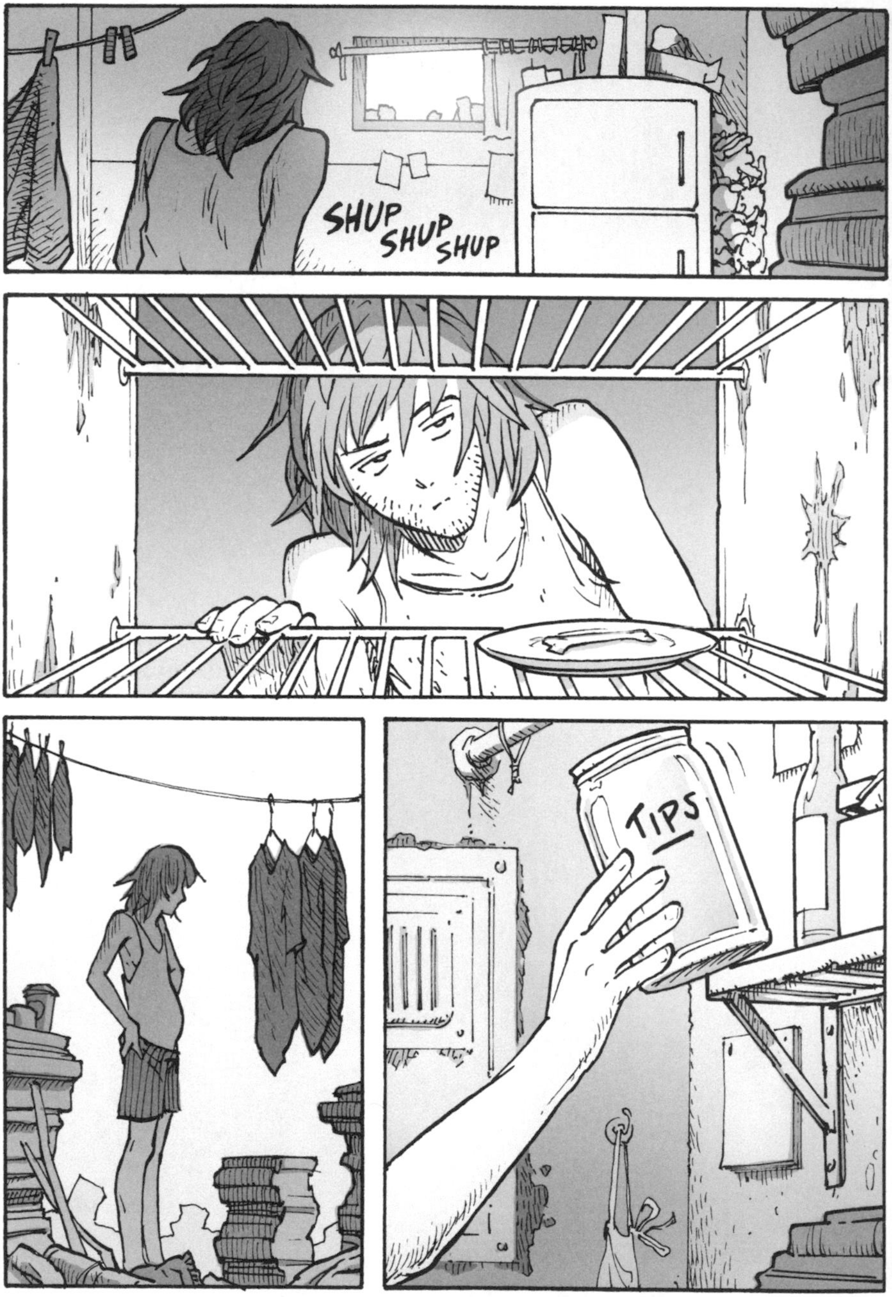
SHUP
SHUP
SHUP
TIPS

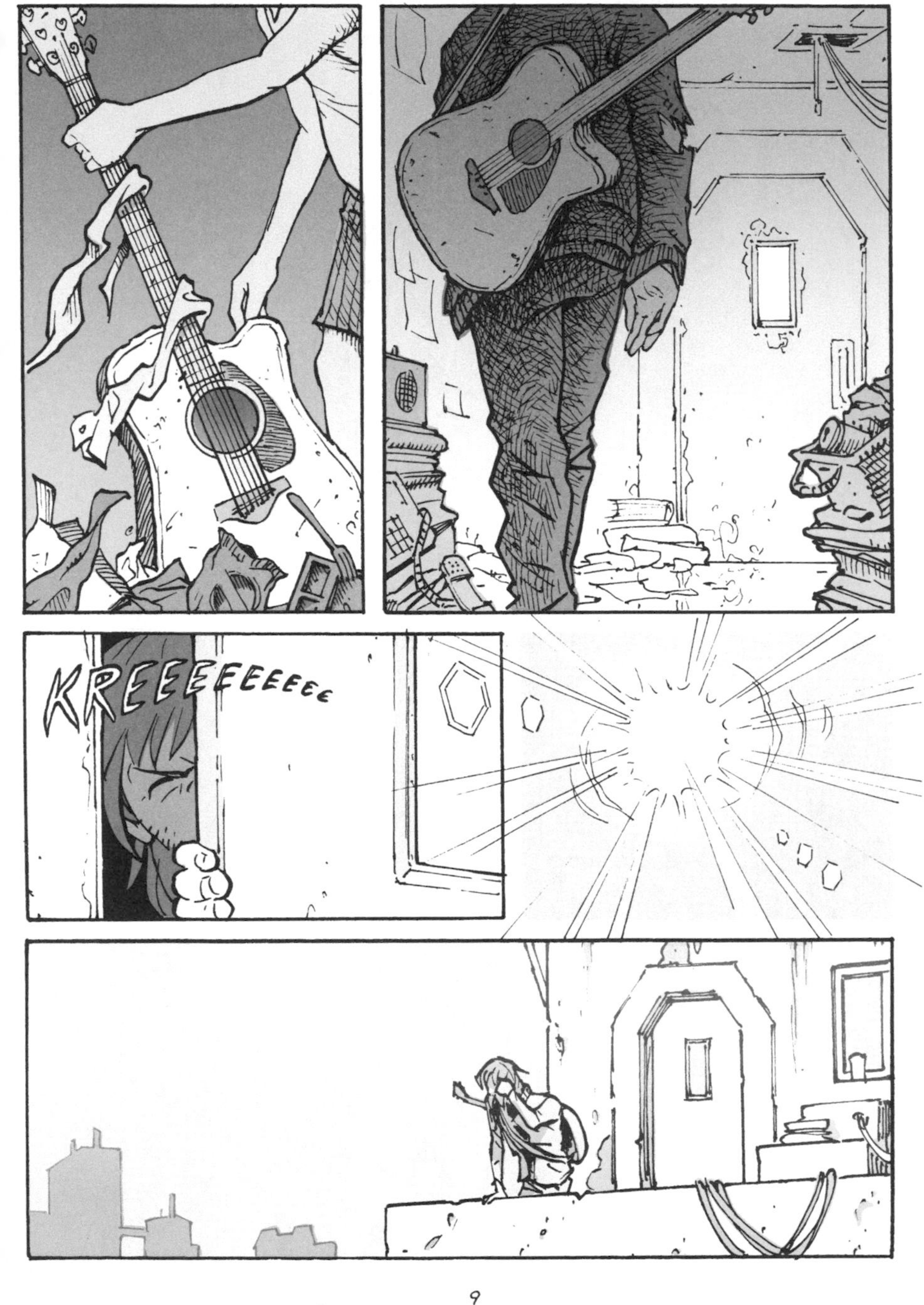
KREEEEEEEEEe

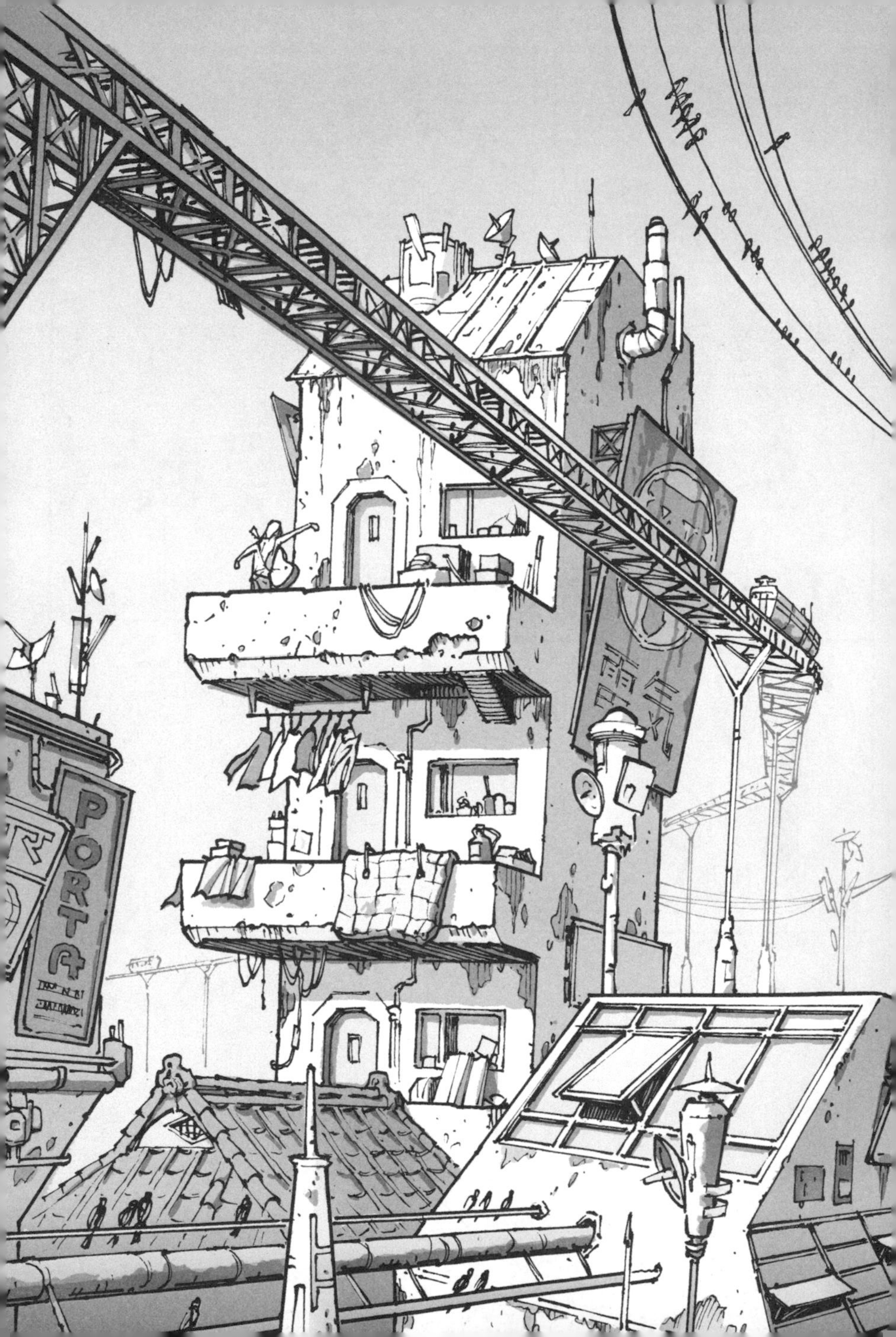
PORTA

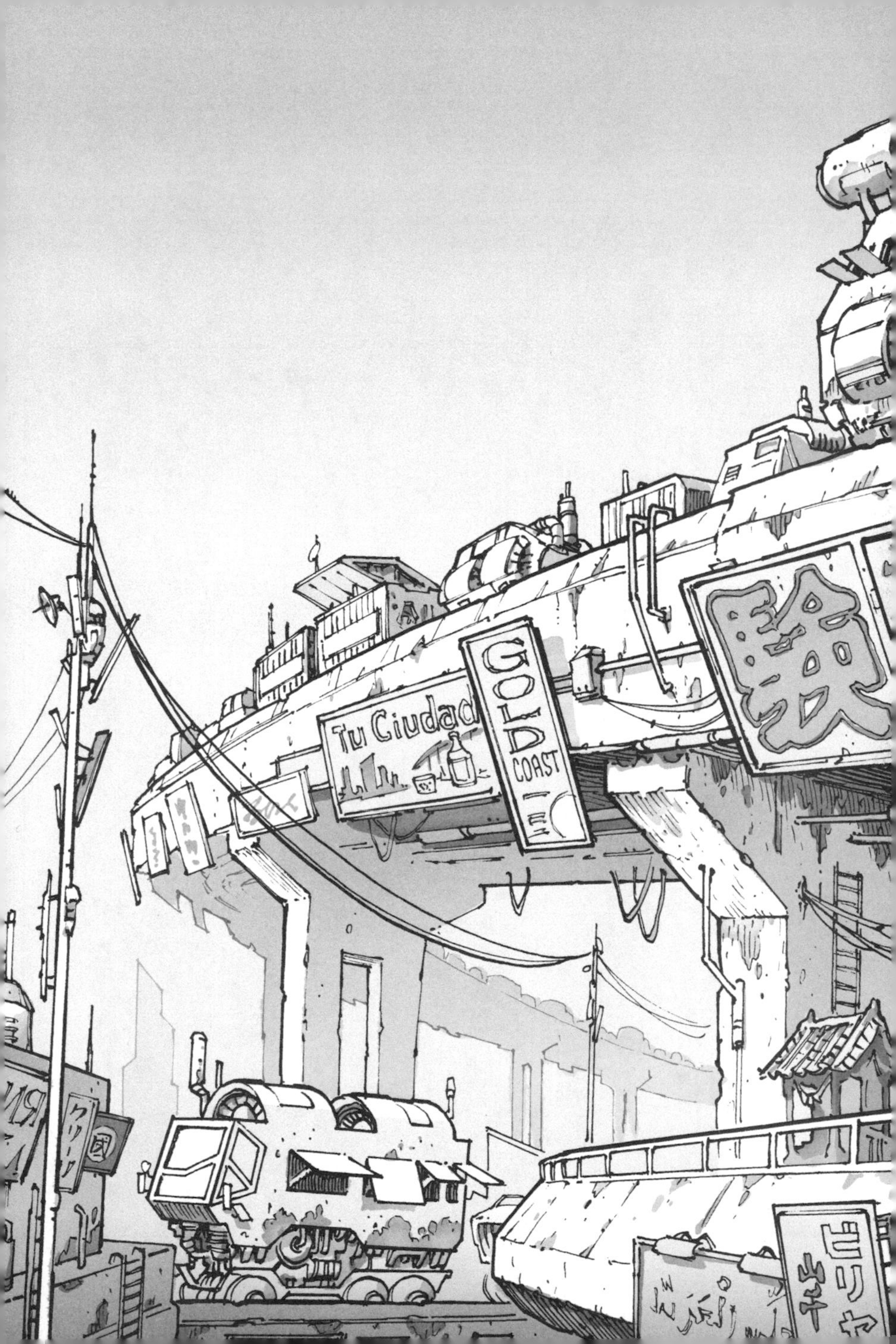
Tu Ciudad
GOLD COAST

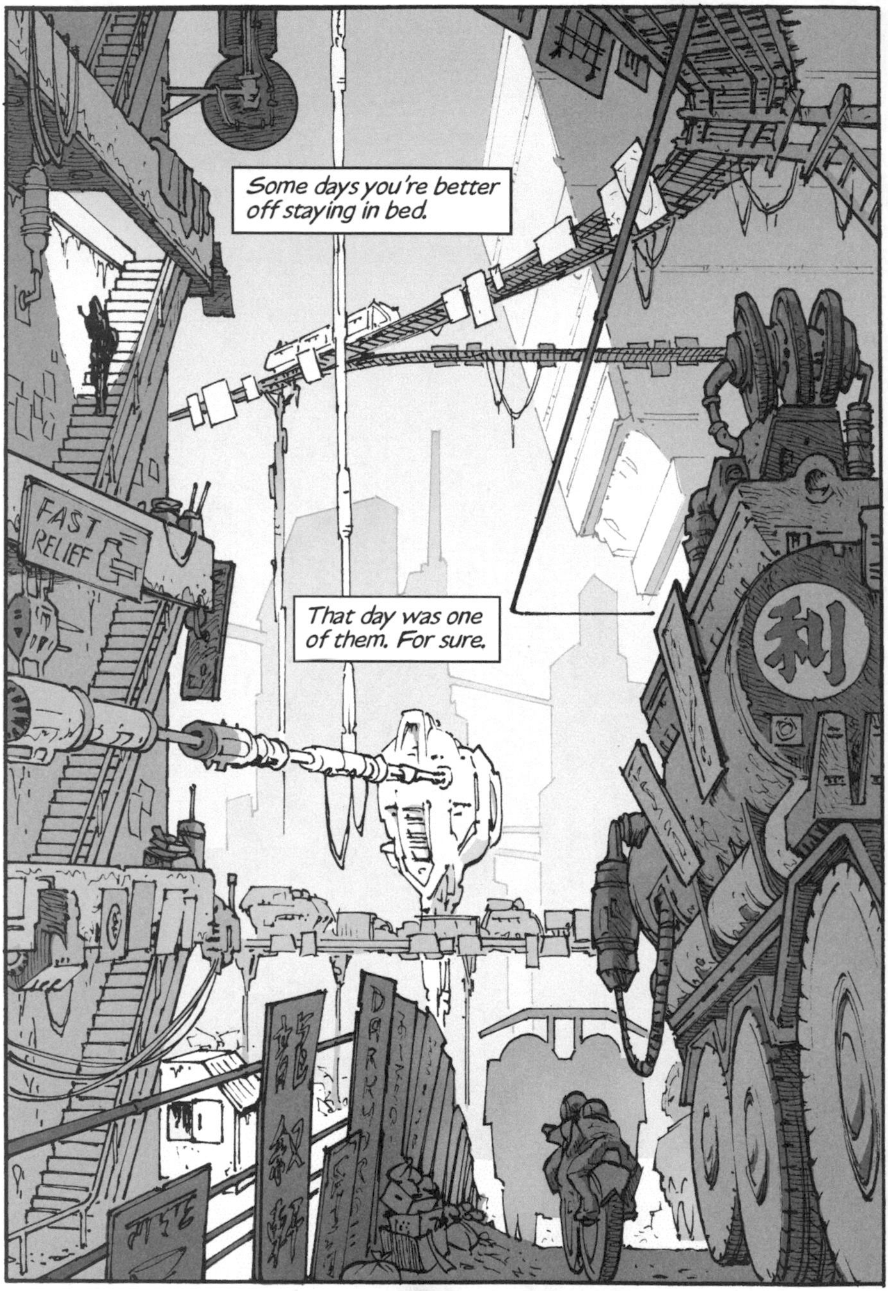
Some days you're better off staying in bed.
That day was one of them. For sure.
FAST RELIEF
利

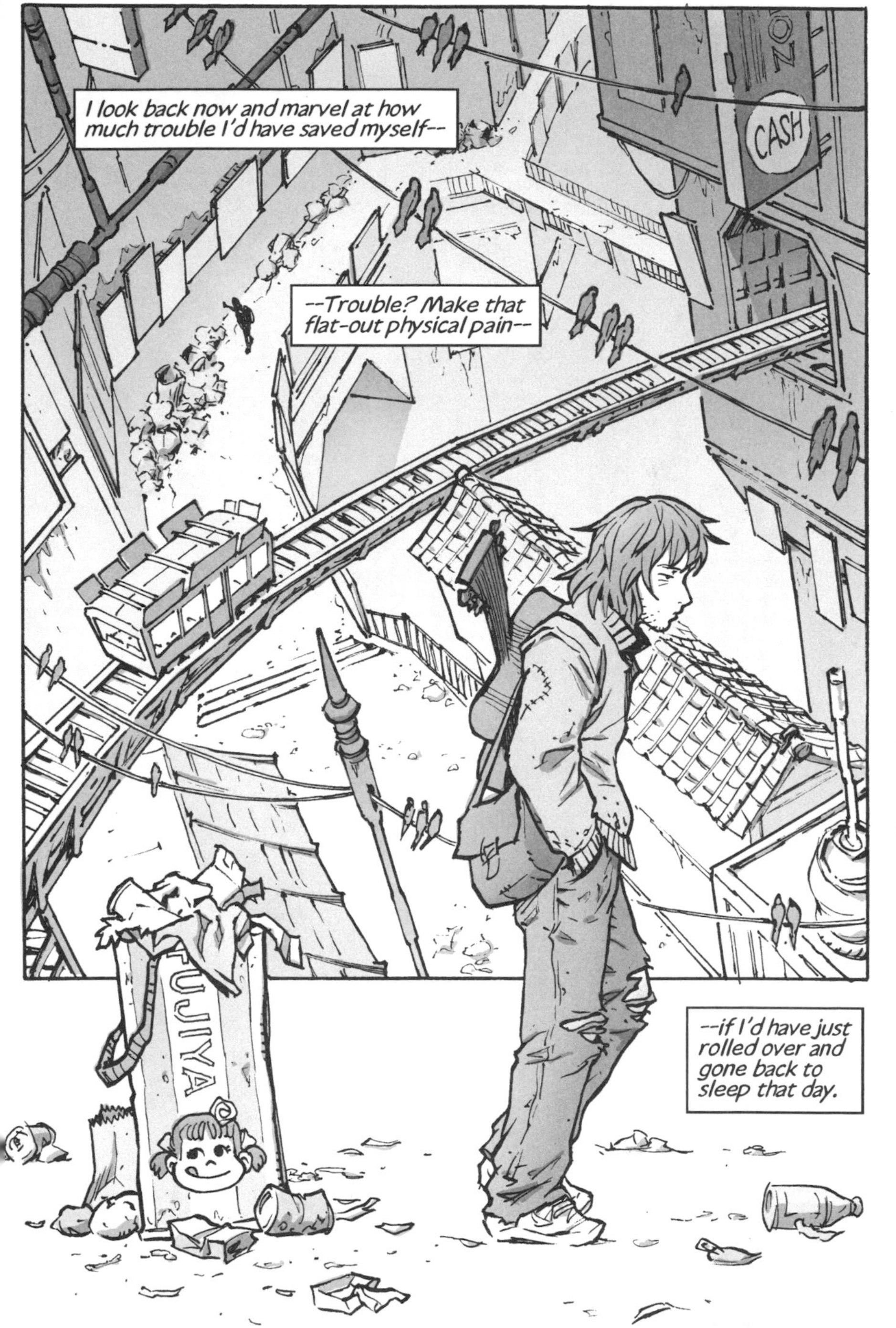
I look back now and marvel at how much trouble I'd have saved myself--
CASH
--Trouble? Make that flat-out physical pain--
FUJIYA
--if I'd have just rolled over and gone back to sleep that day.

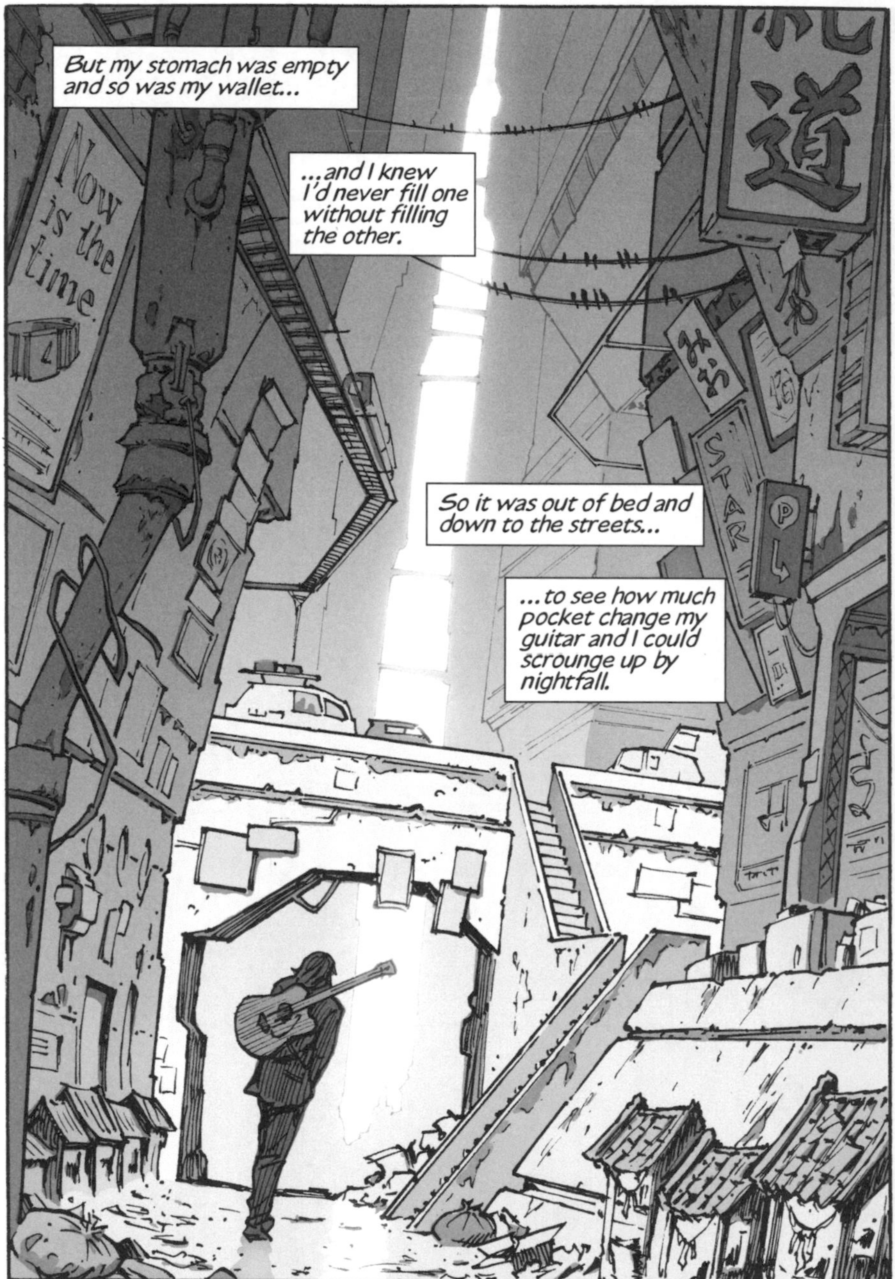
But my stomach was empty and so was my wallet...
...and I knew I'd never fill one without filling the other.
Now is the time.
So it was out of bed and down to the streets...
STAR
...to see how much pocket change my guitar and I could scrounge up by nightfall.

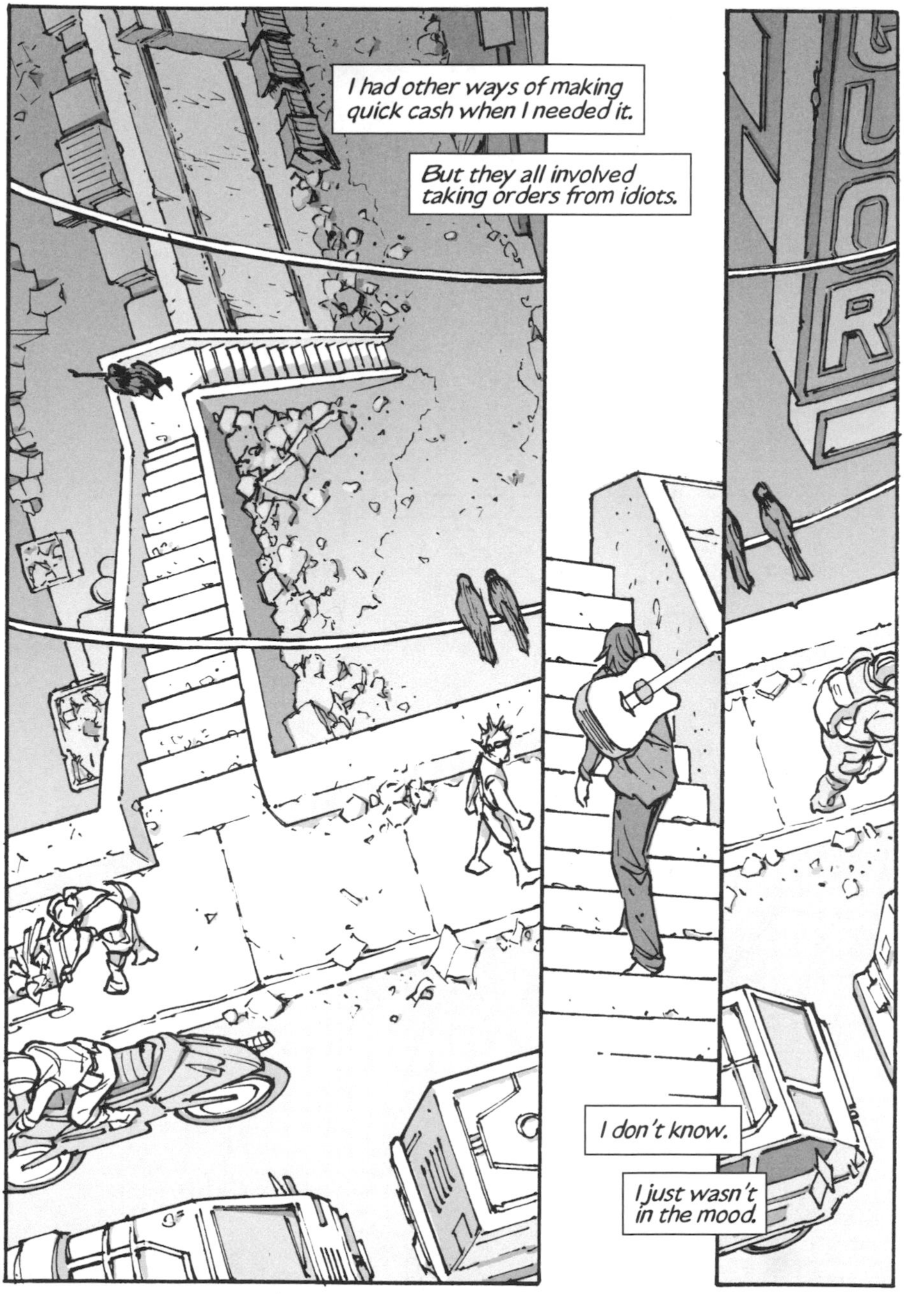
I had other ways of making quick cash when I needed it.
But they all involved taking orders from idiots.
I don't know.
I just wasn't in the mood.

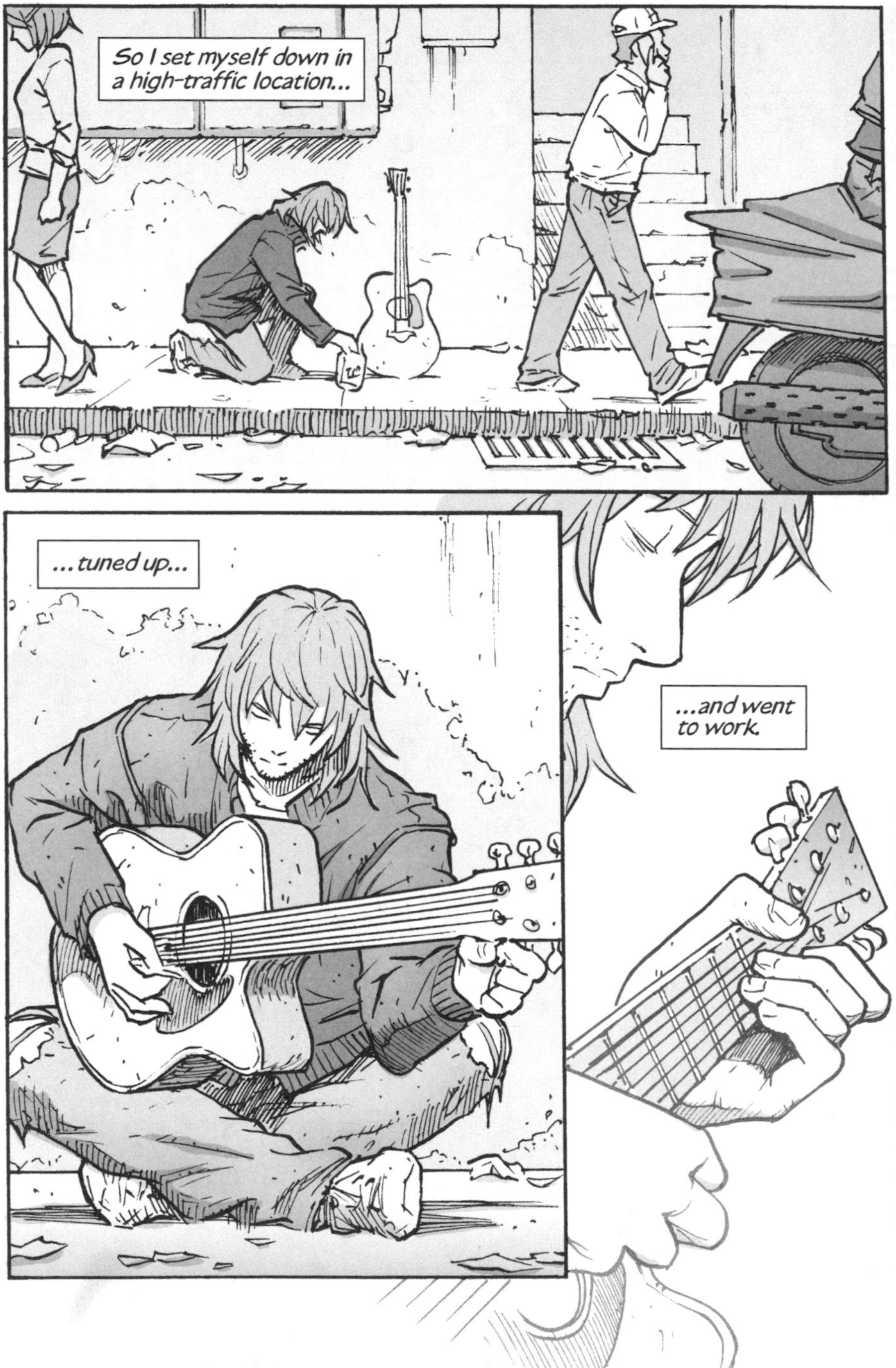
So I set myself down in a high-traffic location...
...tuned up...
...and went to work.

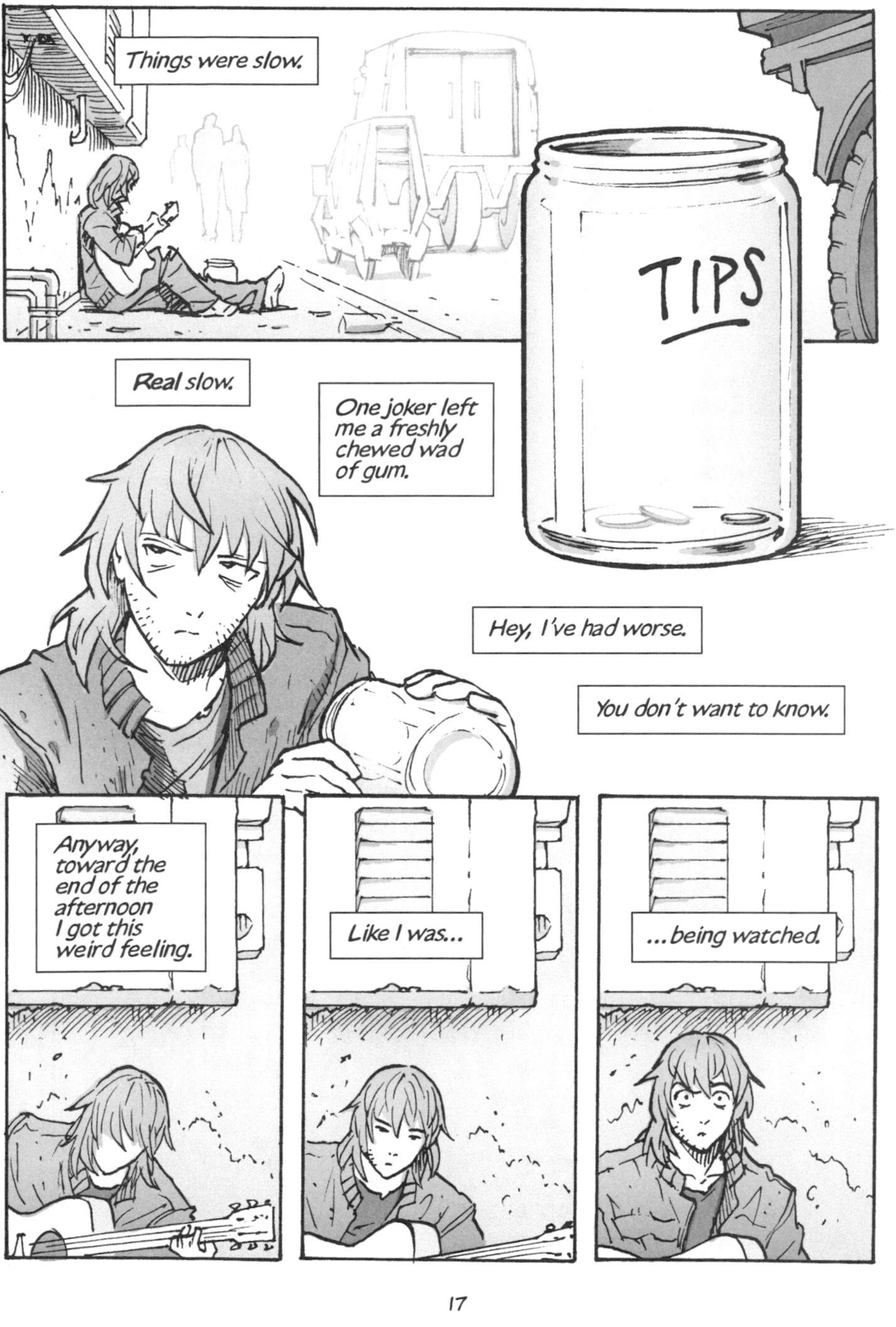
Things were slow.
TIPS
Real slow.
One joker left me a freshly chewed wad of gum.
Hey, I've had worse.
You don't want to know.
Anyway, toward the end of the afternoon I got this weird feeling.
Like I was...
...being watched.

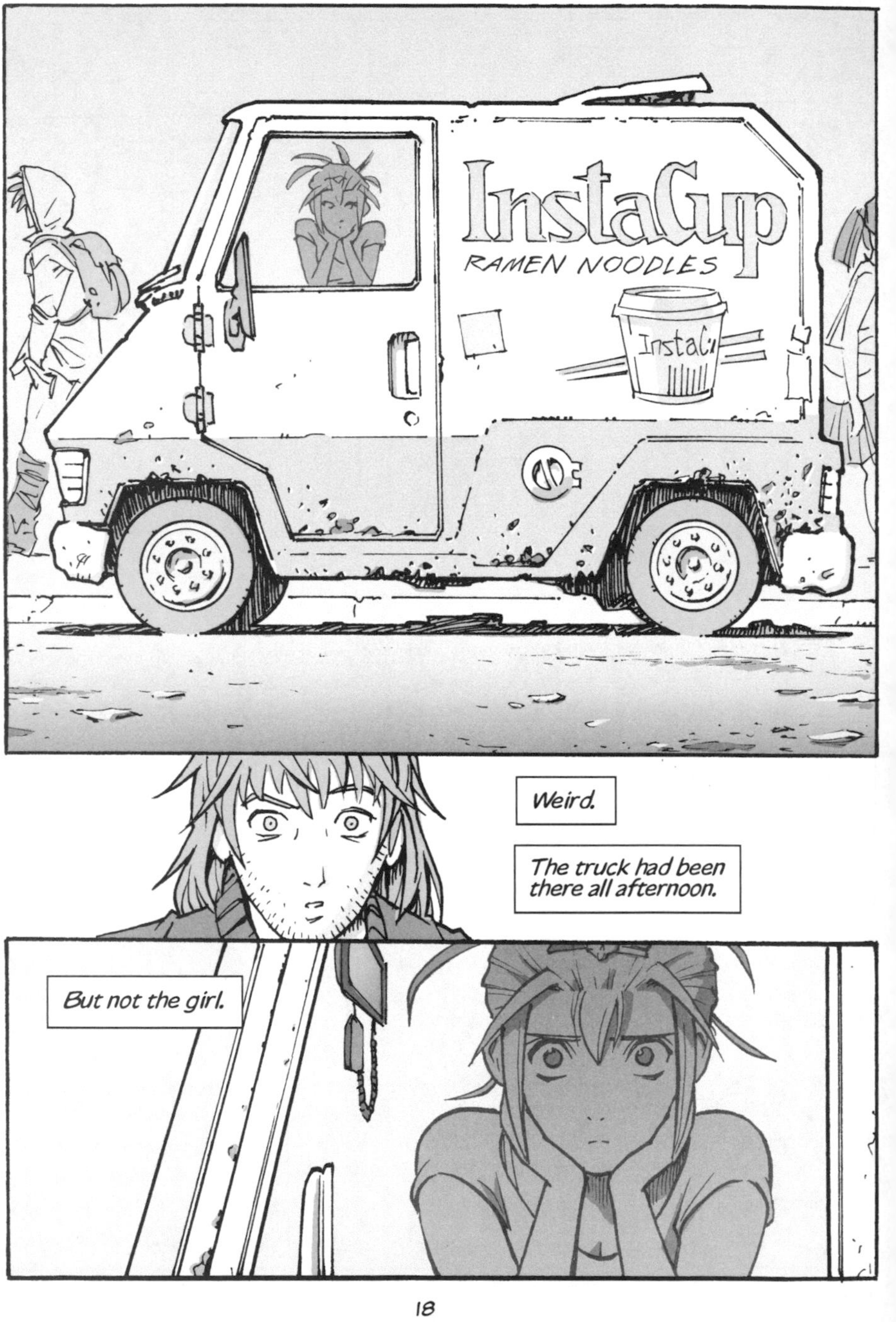
InstaCup
RAMEN NOODLES
Weird.
The truck had been there all afternoon.
But not the girl.

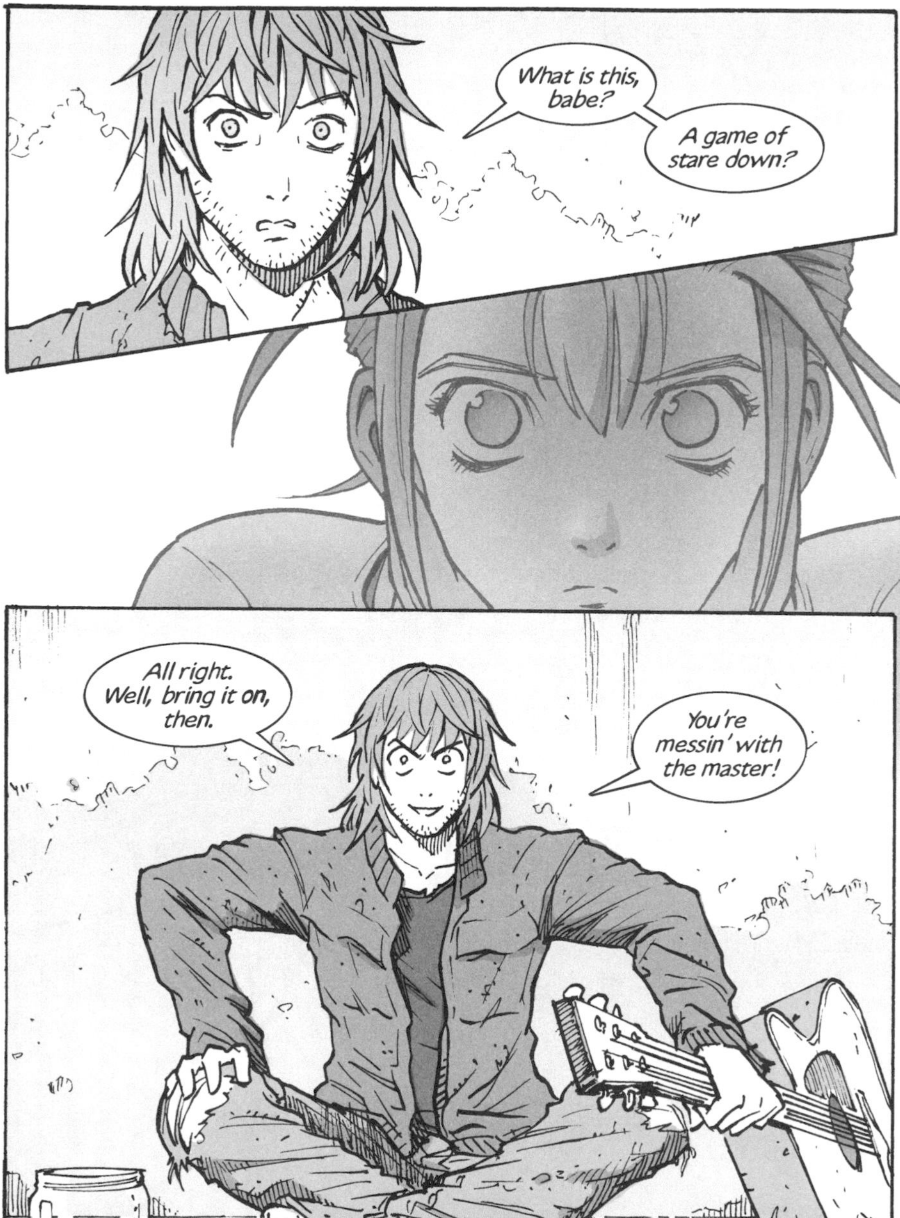
What is this, babe?
A game of stare down?
All right. Well, bring it on, then.
You're messin' with the master!
TIPS

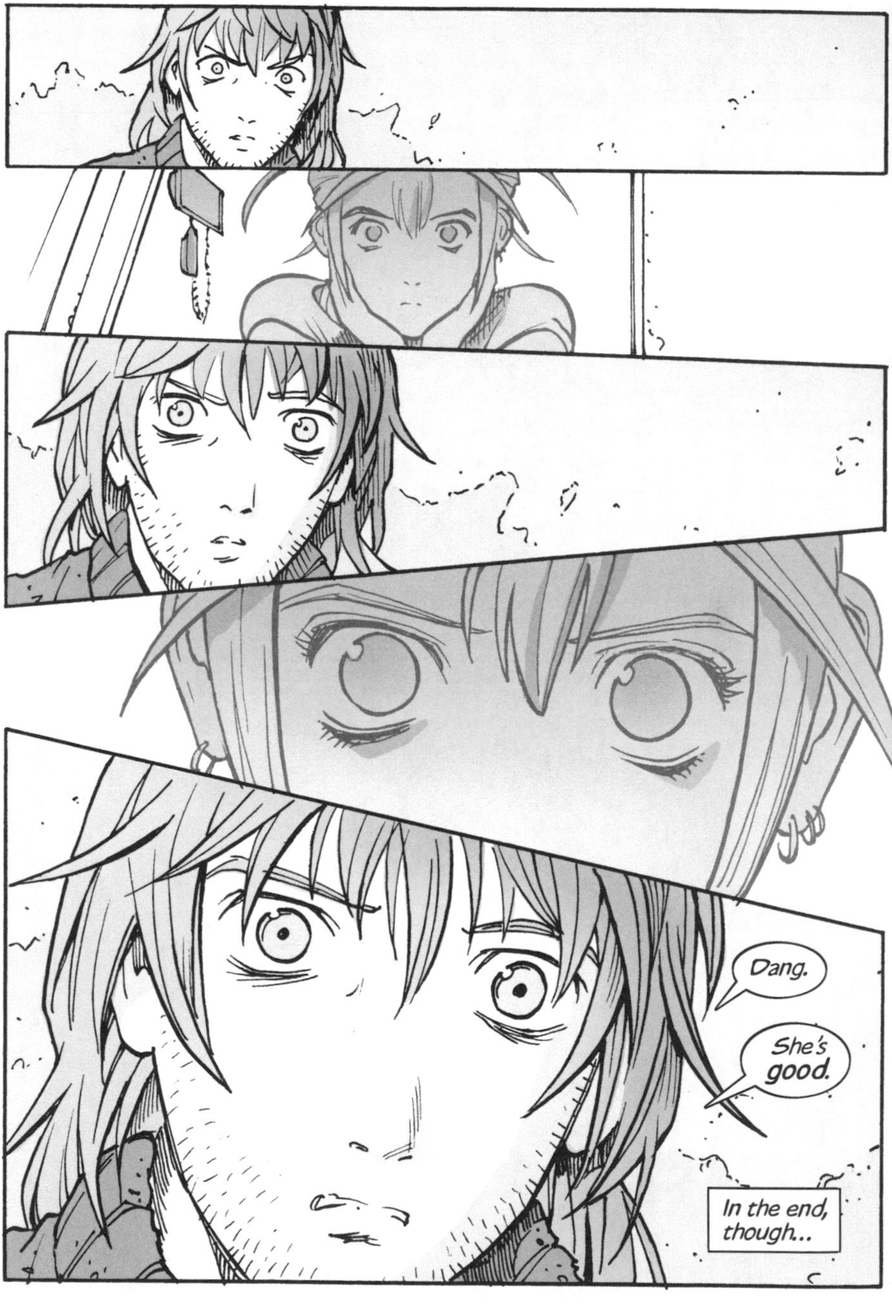
Dang.
She's good.
In the end, though...

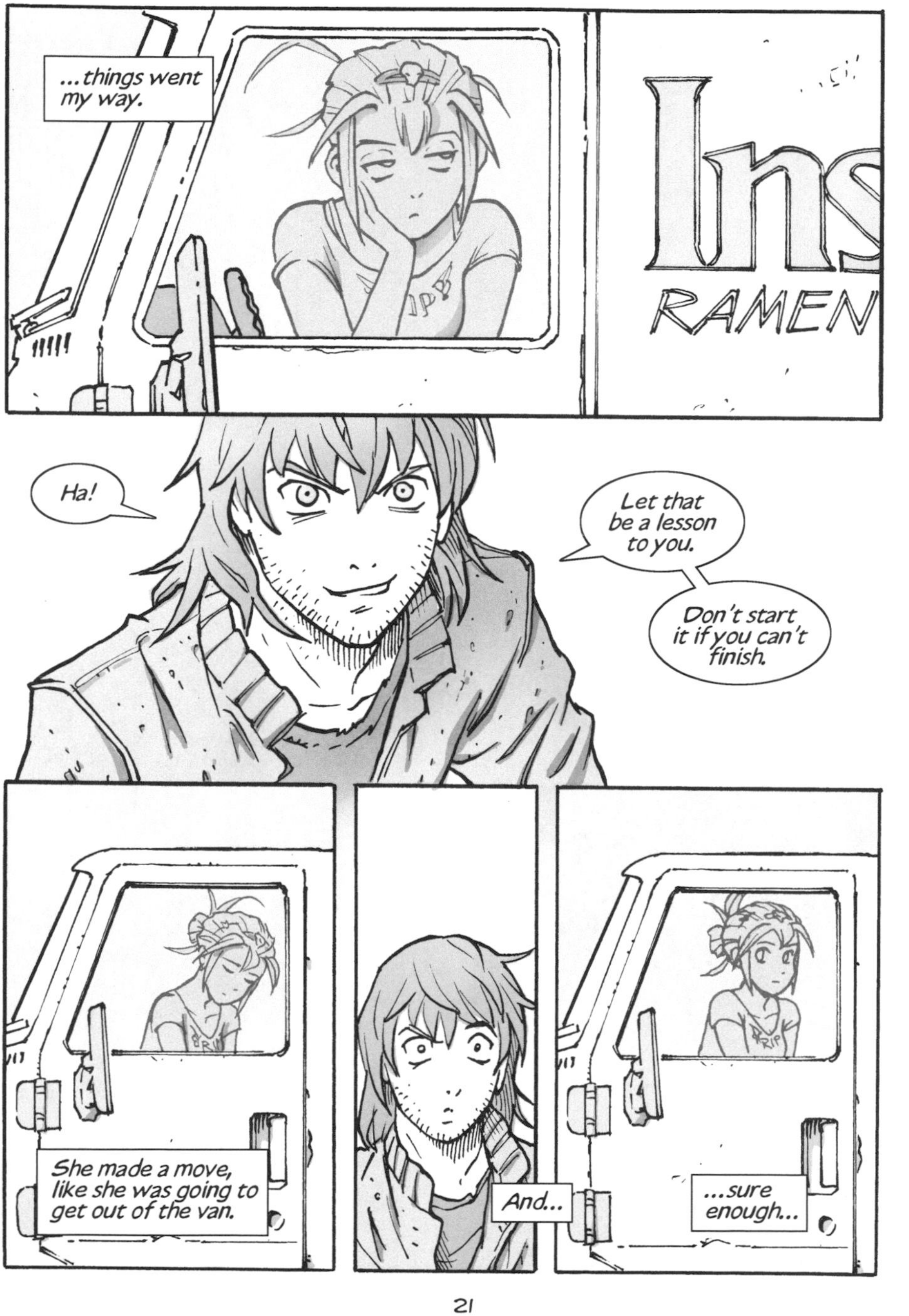
...things went my way.
Ins
RAMEN
Ha!
Let that be a lesson to you.
Don't start it if you can't finish.
She made a move, like she was going to get out of the van.
And...
...sure enough...

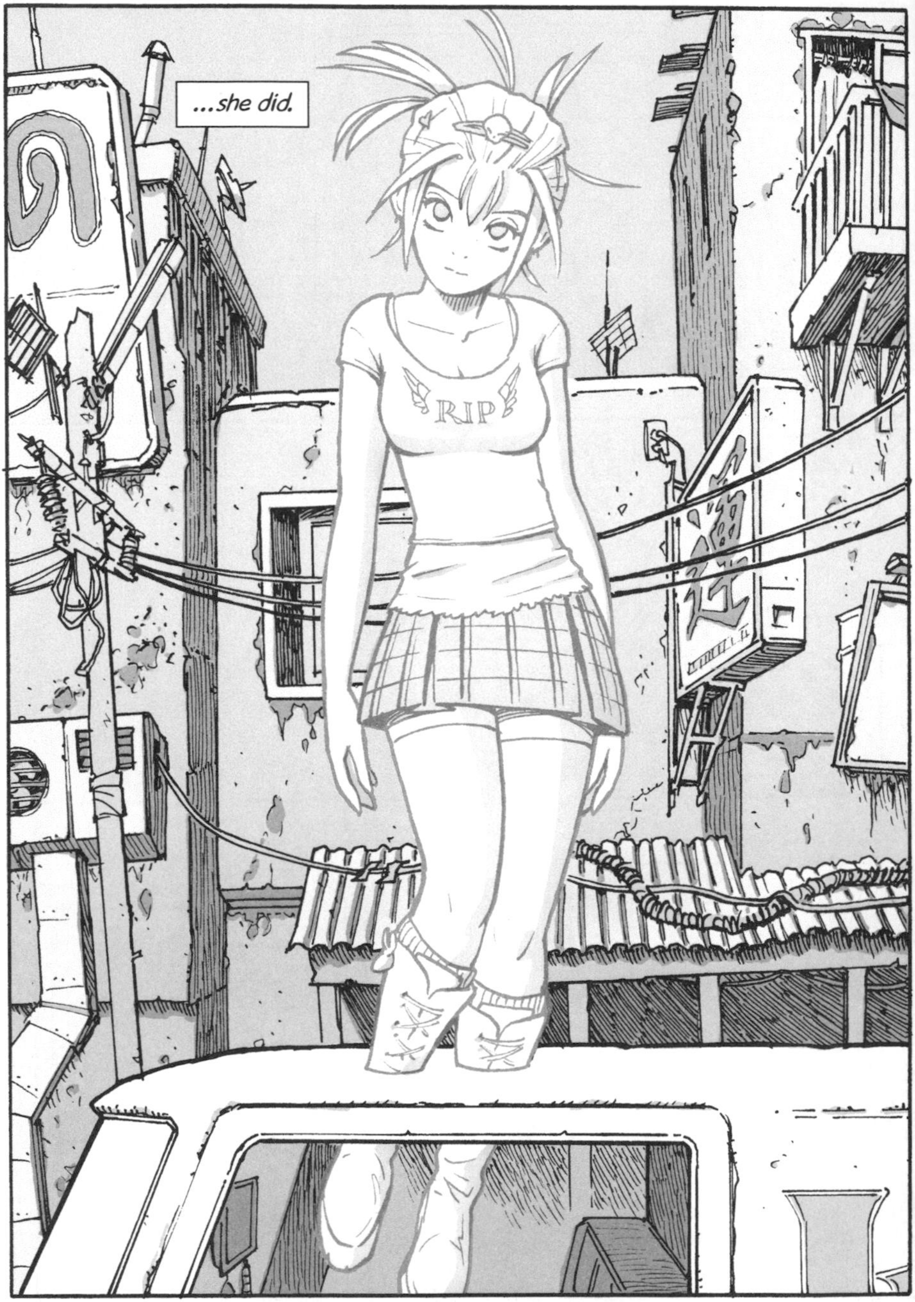
...she did.
RIP

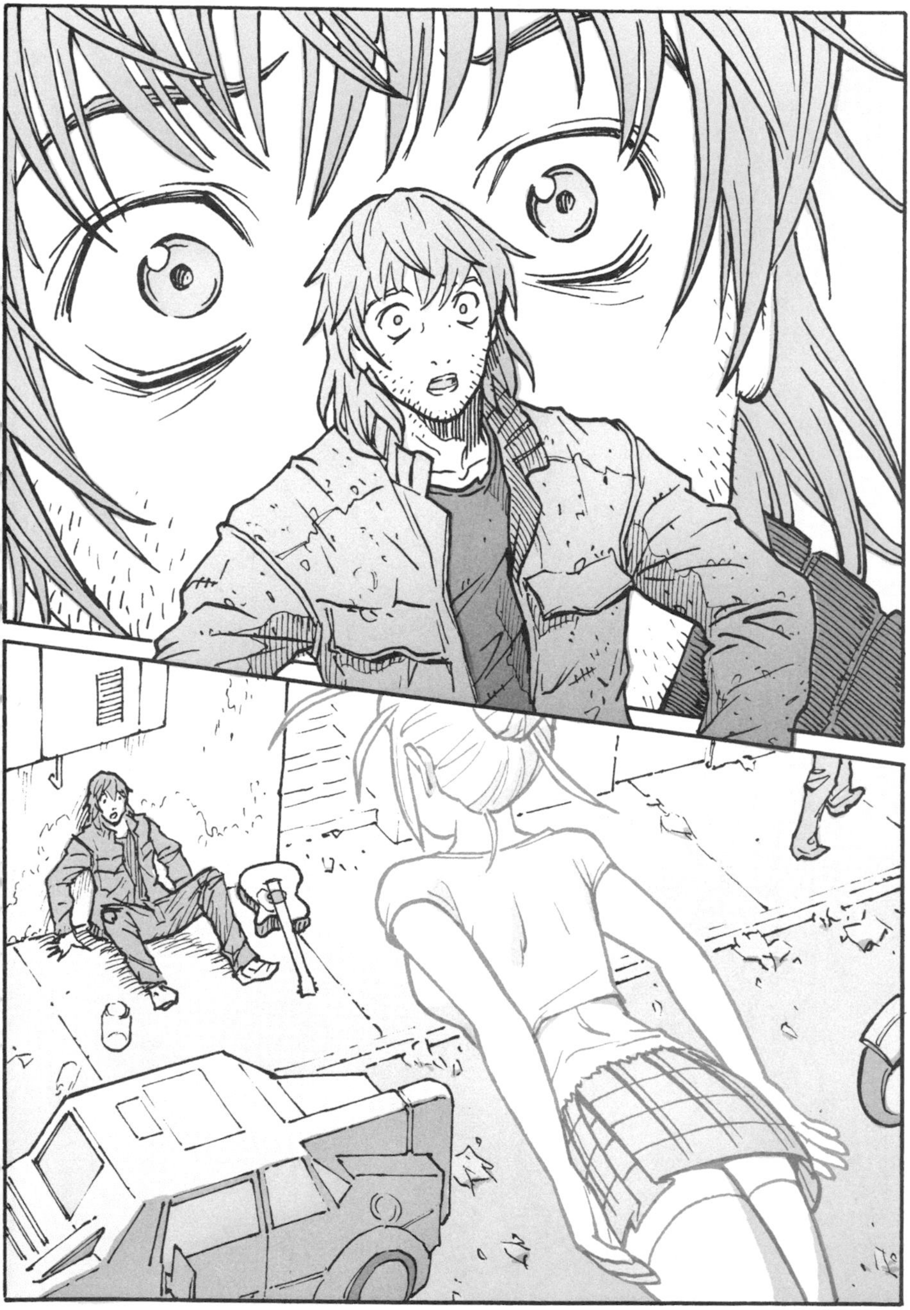

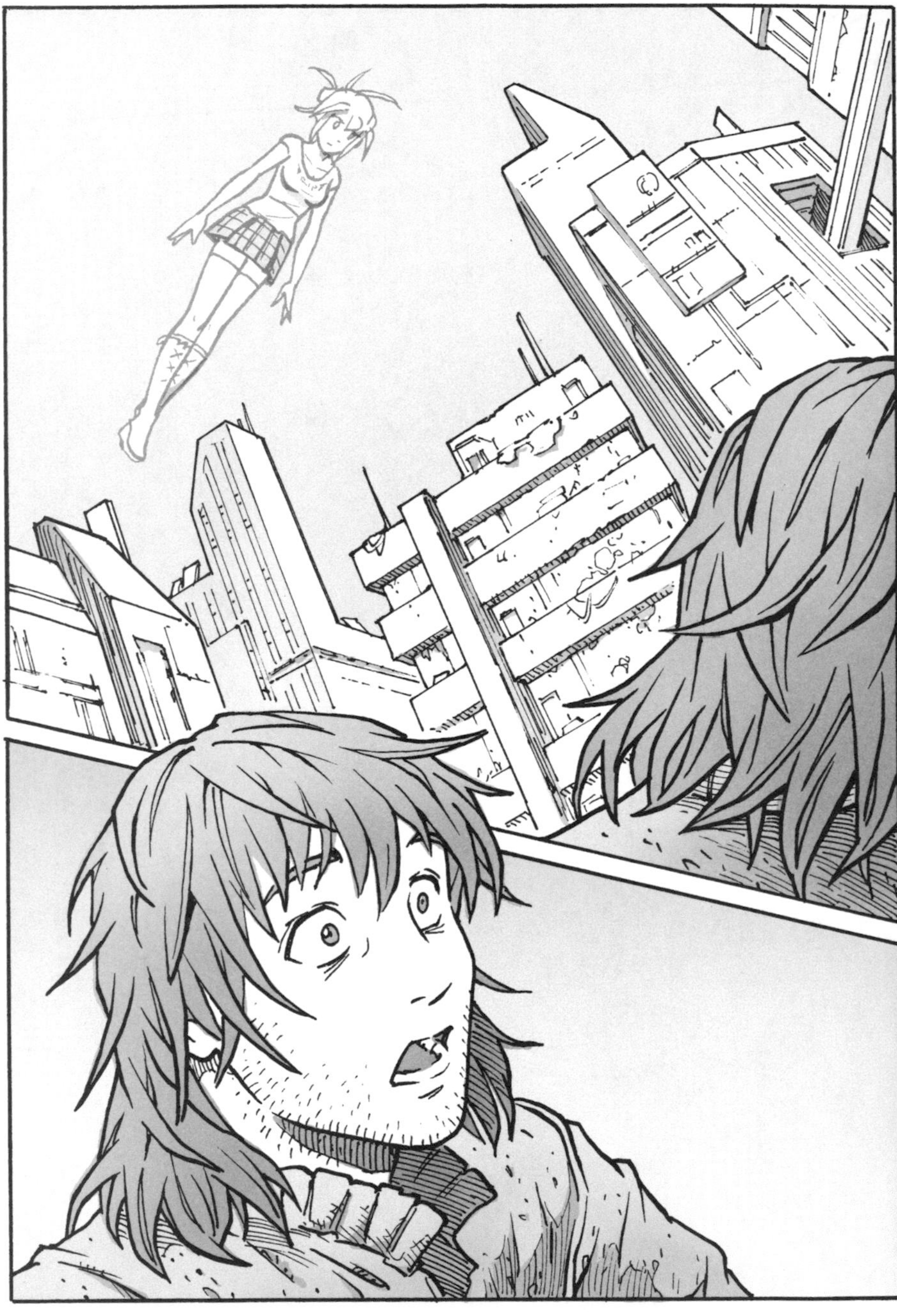

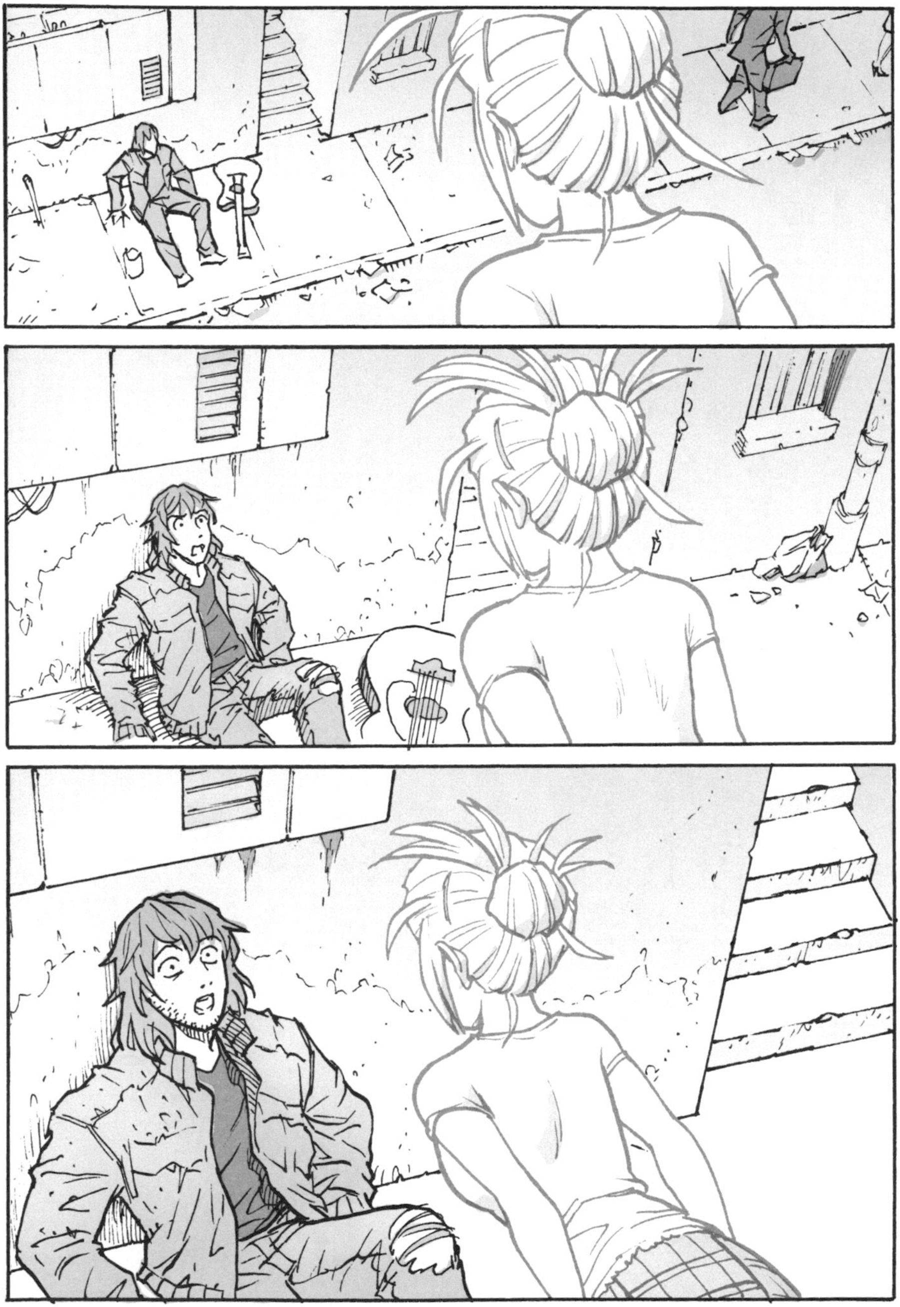

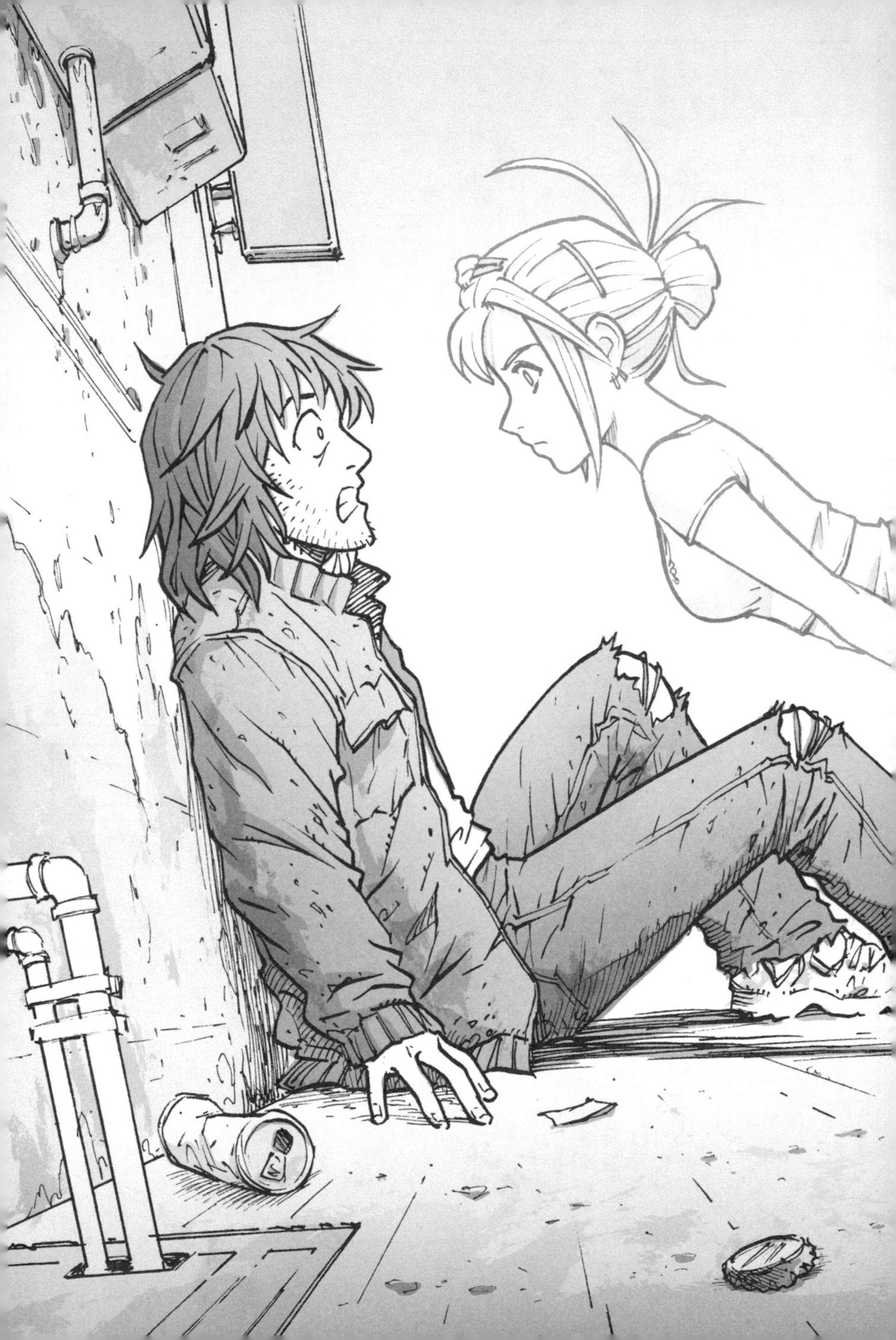

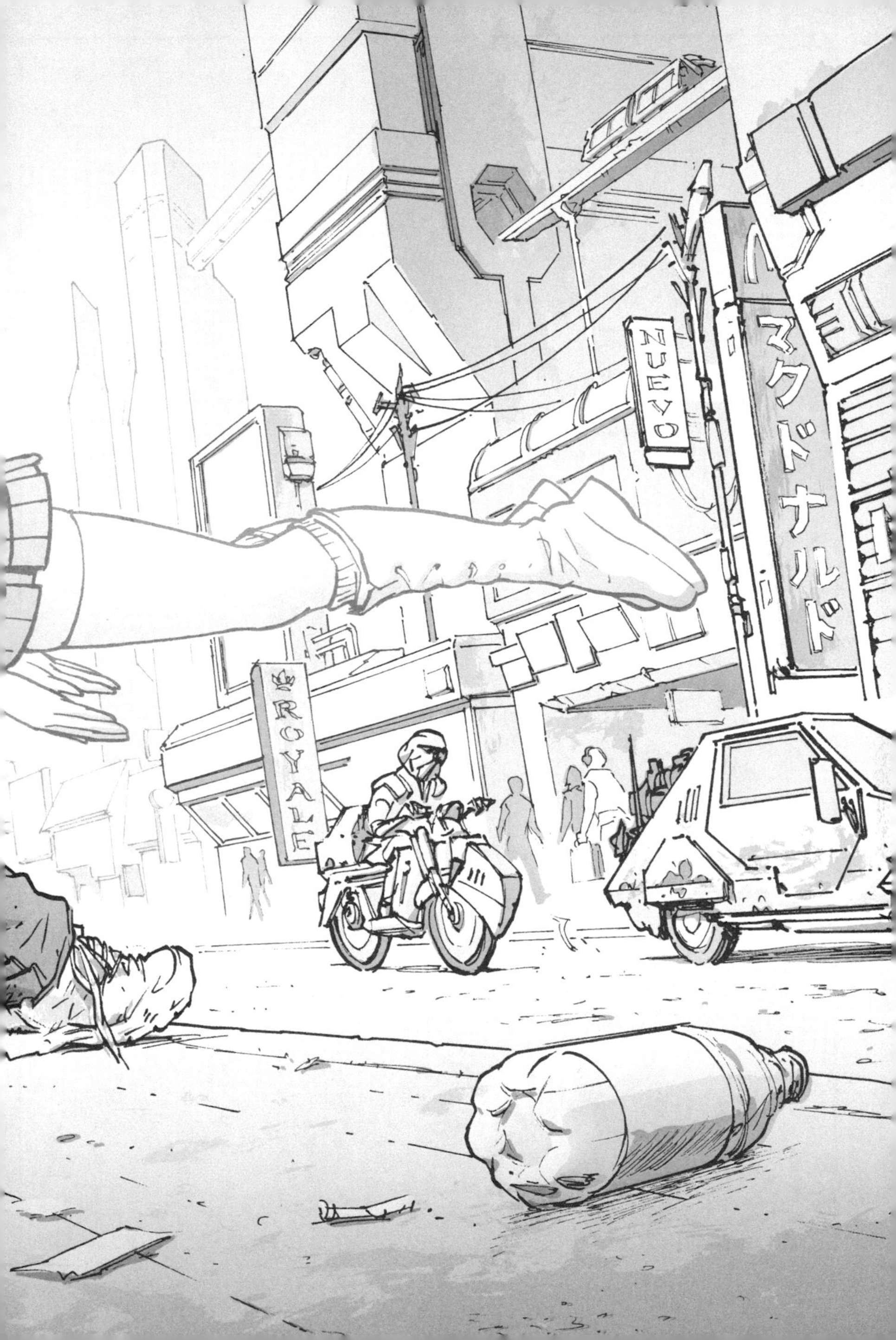
NUEVO
マクドナルド
ROYALE

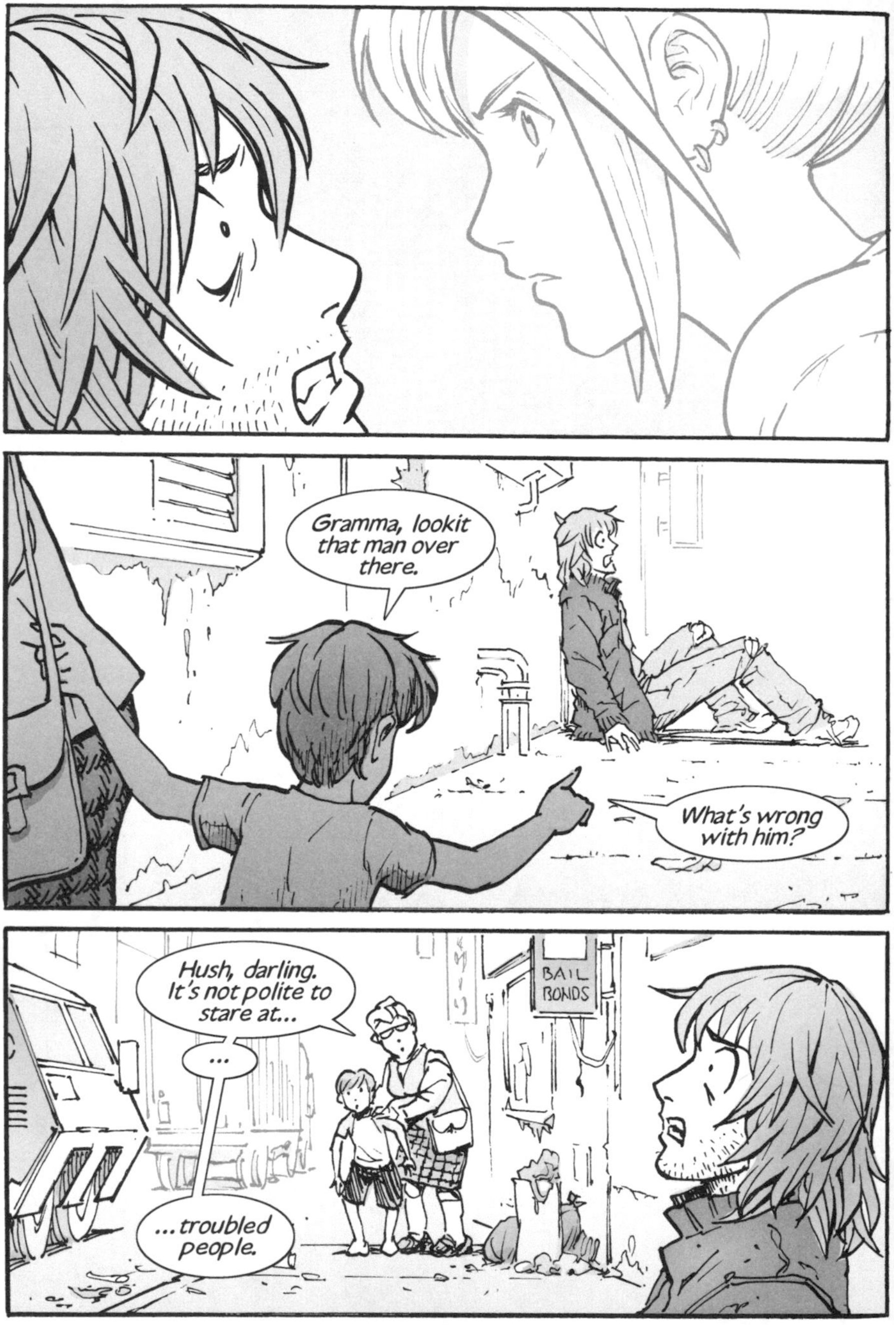
Gramma, lookit that man over there.
What's wrong with him?
Hush, darling. It's not polite to stare at...
...
...troubled people.
BAIL BONDS

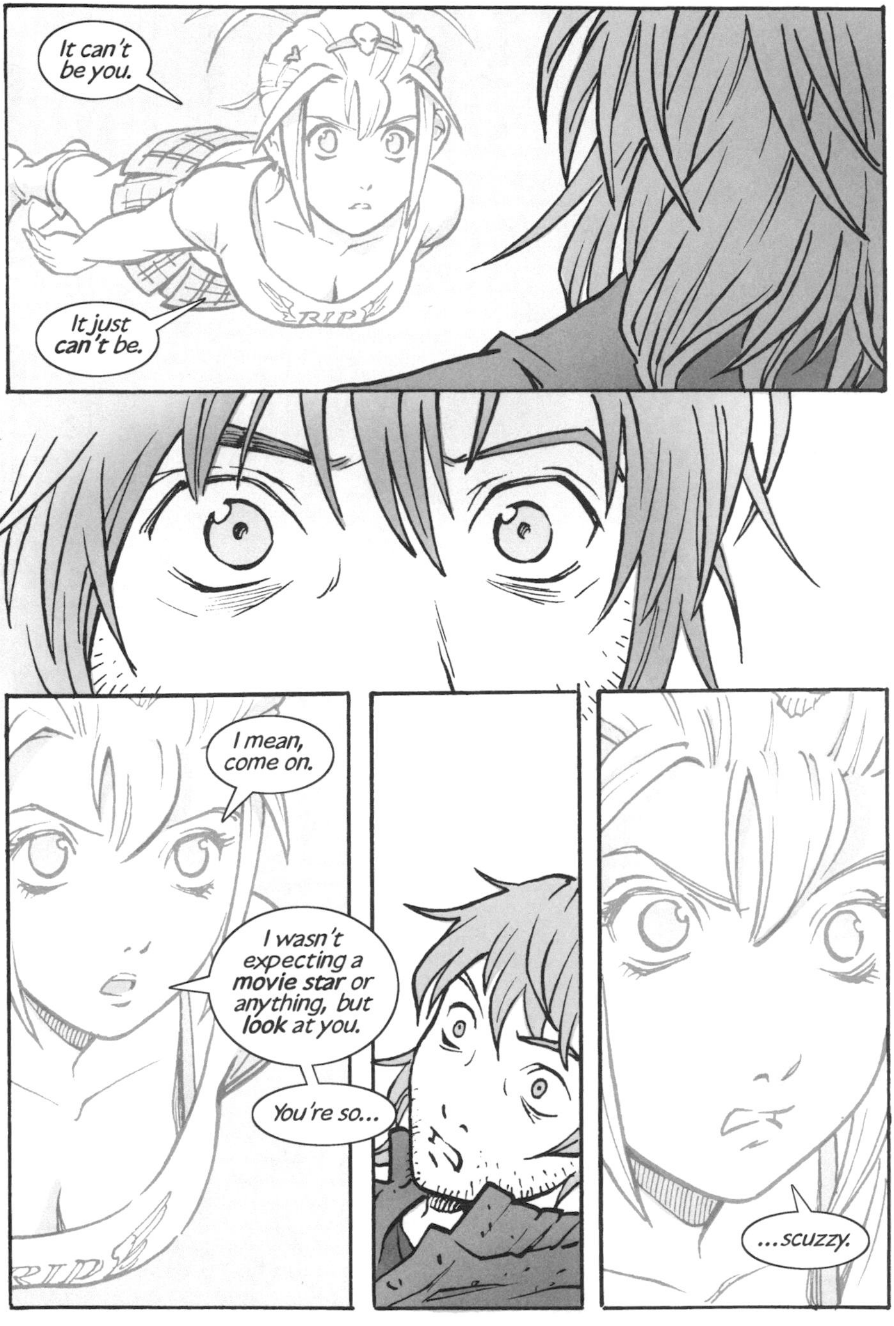
It can't be you.
It just can't be.
RIP
I mean, come on.
I wasn't expecting a **movie star** or anything, but **look** at you.
You're so...
...scuzzy.

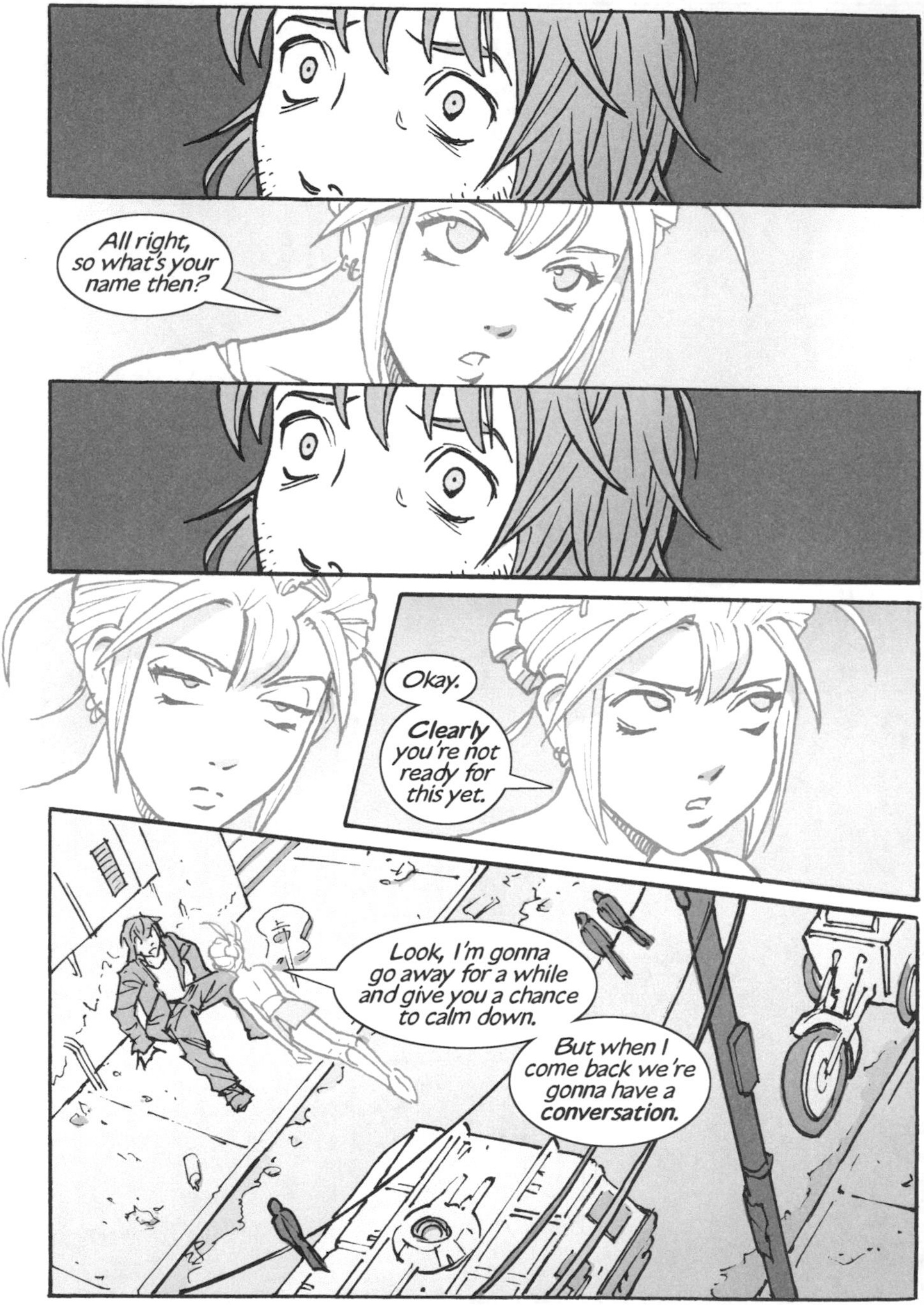
All right, so what's your name then?
Okay.
Clearly you're not ready for this yet.
Look, I'm gonna go away for a while and give you a chance to calm down.
But when I come back we're gonna have a conversation.

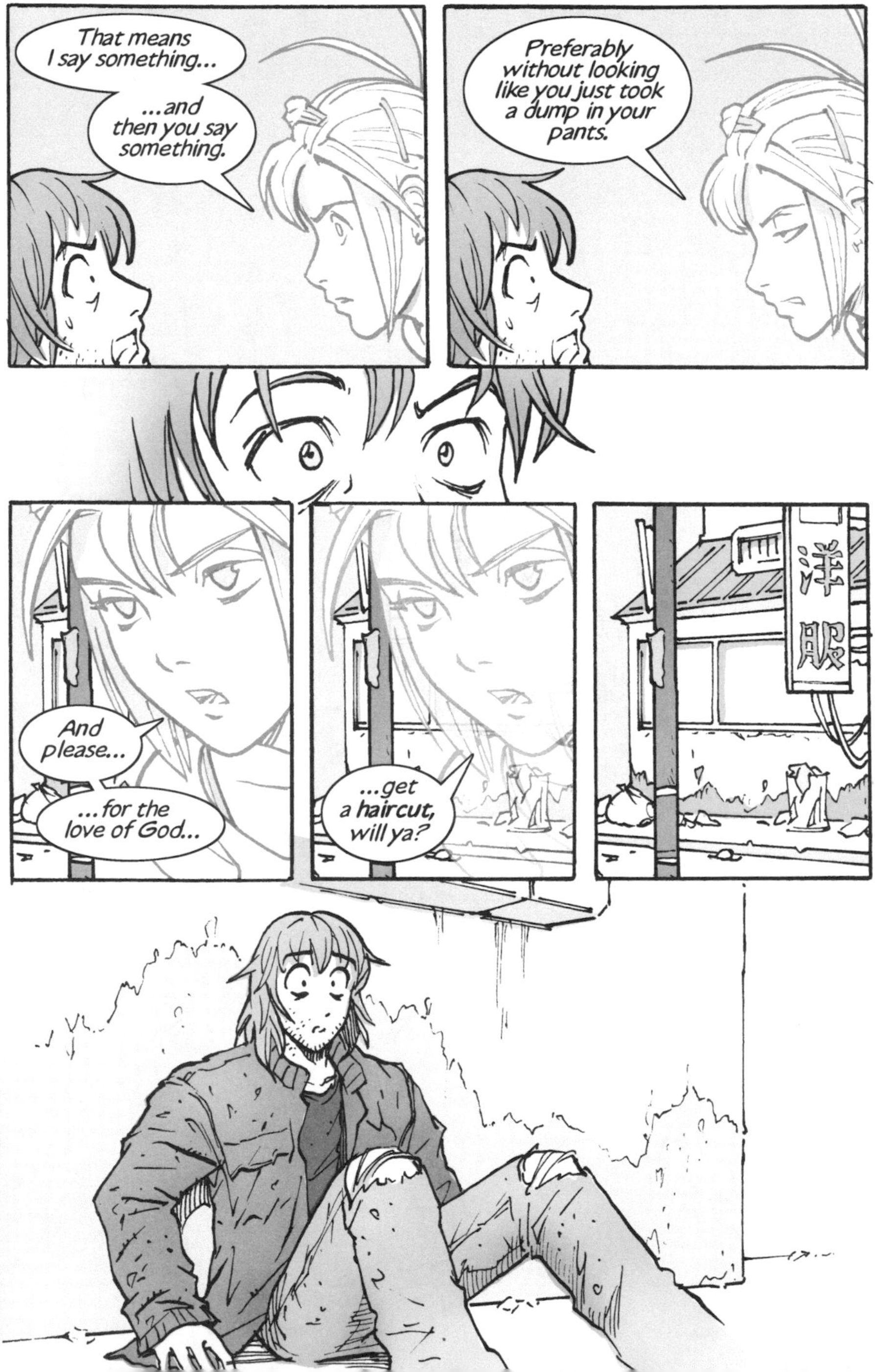
That means I say something...
...and then you say something.
Preferably without looking like you just took a dump in your pants.
And please...
...for the love of God...
...get a **haircut**, will ya?
洋服

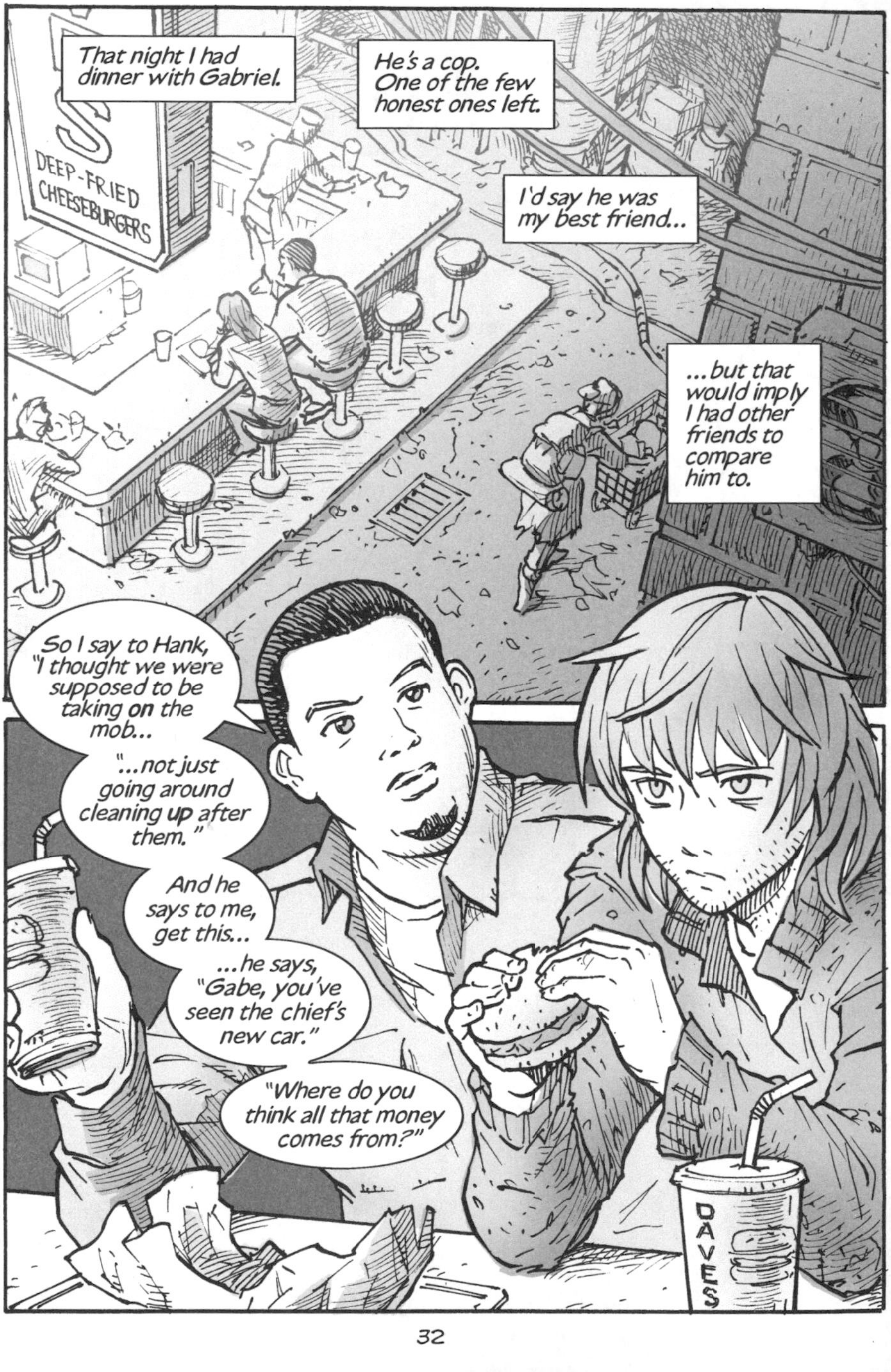
That night I had dinner with Gabriel.
He's a cop. One of the few honest ones left.
DEEP-FRIED CHEESEBURGERS
I'd say he was my best friend...
...but that would imply I had other friends to compare him to.
So I say to Hank, "I thought we were supposed to be taking **on** the mob...
"...not just going around cleaning **up** after them."
And he says to me, get this...
...he says, "Gabe, you've seen the chief's new car."
"Where do you think all that money comes from?"
DAVES

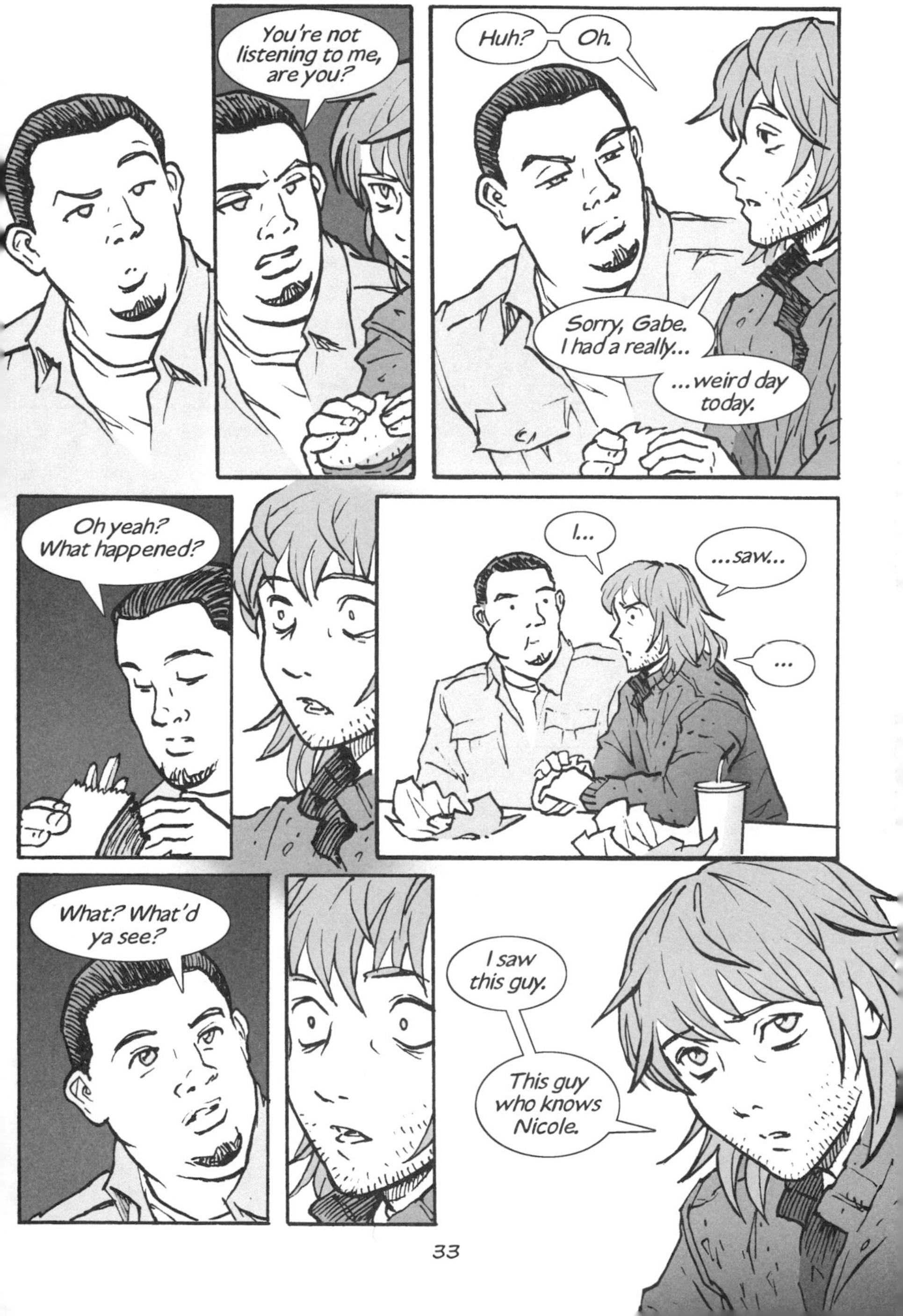
You're not listening to me, are you?
Huh?
Oh.
Sorry, Gabe. I had a really...
...weird day today.
Oh yeah? What happened?
I...
...saw...
...
What? What'd ya see?
I saw this guy.
This guy who knows Nicole.

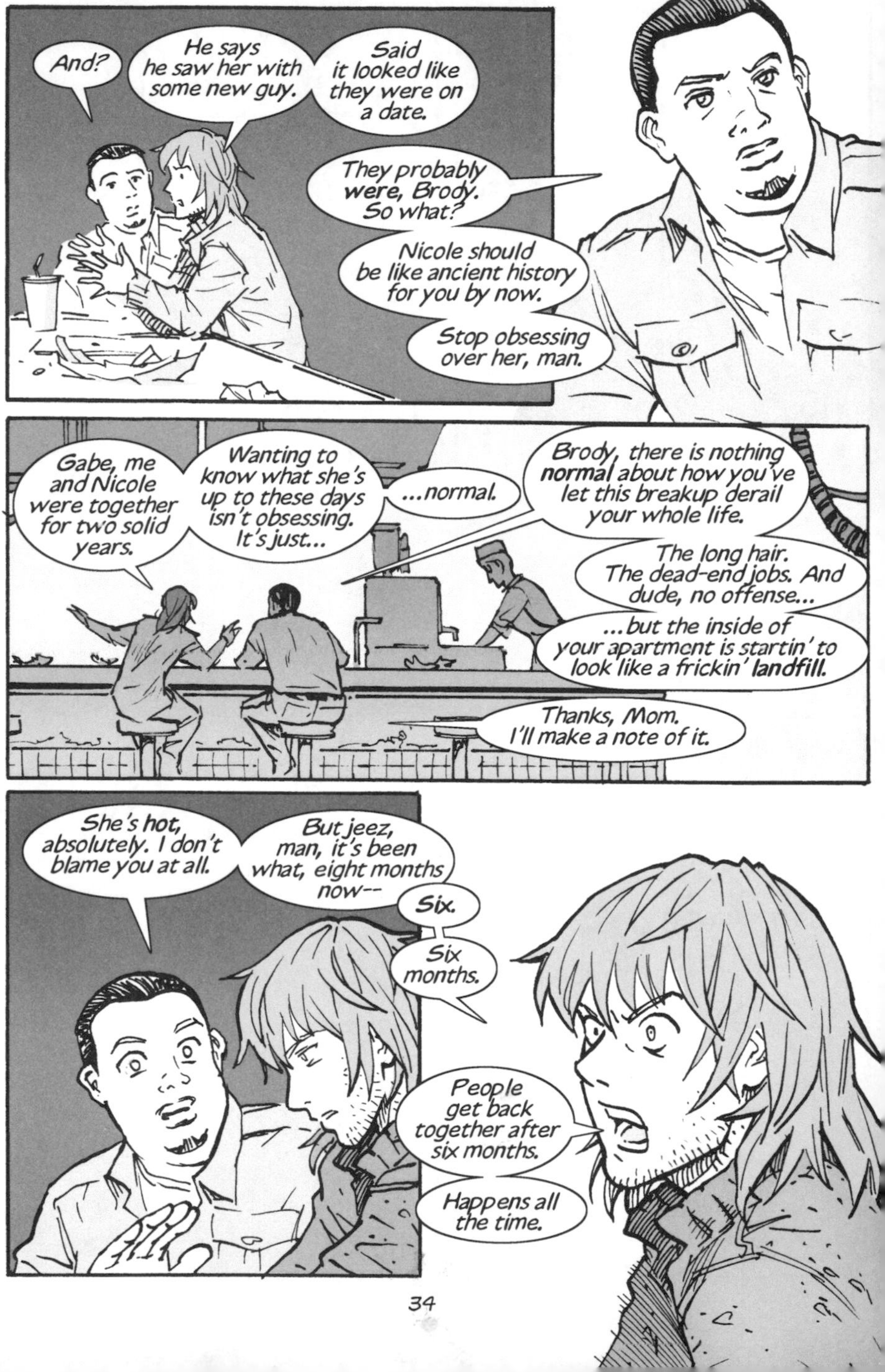
And?
He says he saw her with some new guy.
Said it looked like they were on a date.
They probably were, Brody. So what?
Nicole should be like ancient history for you by now.
Stop obsessing over her, man.
Gabe, me and Nicole were together for two solid years.
Wanting to know what she's up to these days isn't obsessing. It's just...
...normal.
Brody, there is nothing normal about how you've let this breakup derail your whole life.
The long hair. The dead-end jobs. And dude, no offense...
...but the inside of your apartment is startin' to look like a frickin' landfill.
Thanks, Mom. I'll make a note of it.
She's hot, absolutely. I don't blame you at all.
But jeez, man, it's been what, eight months now--
Six.
Six months.
People get back together after six months.
Happens all the time.

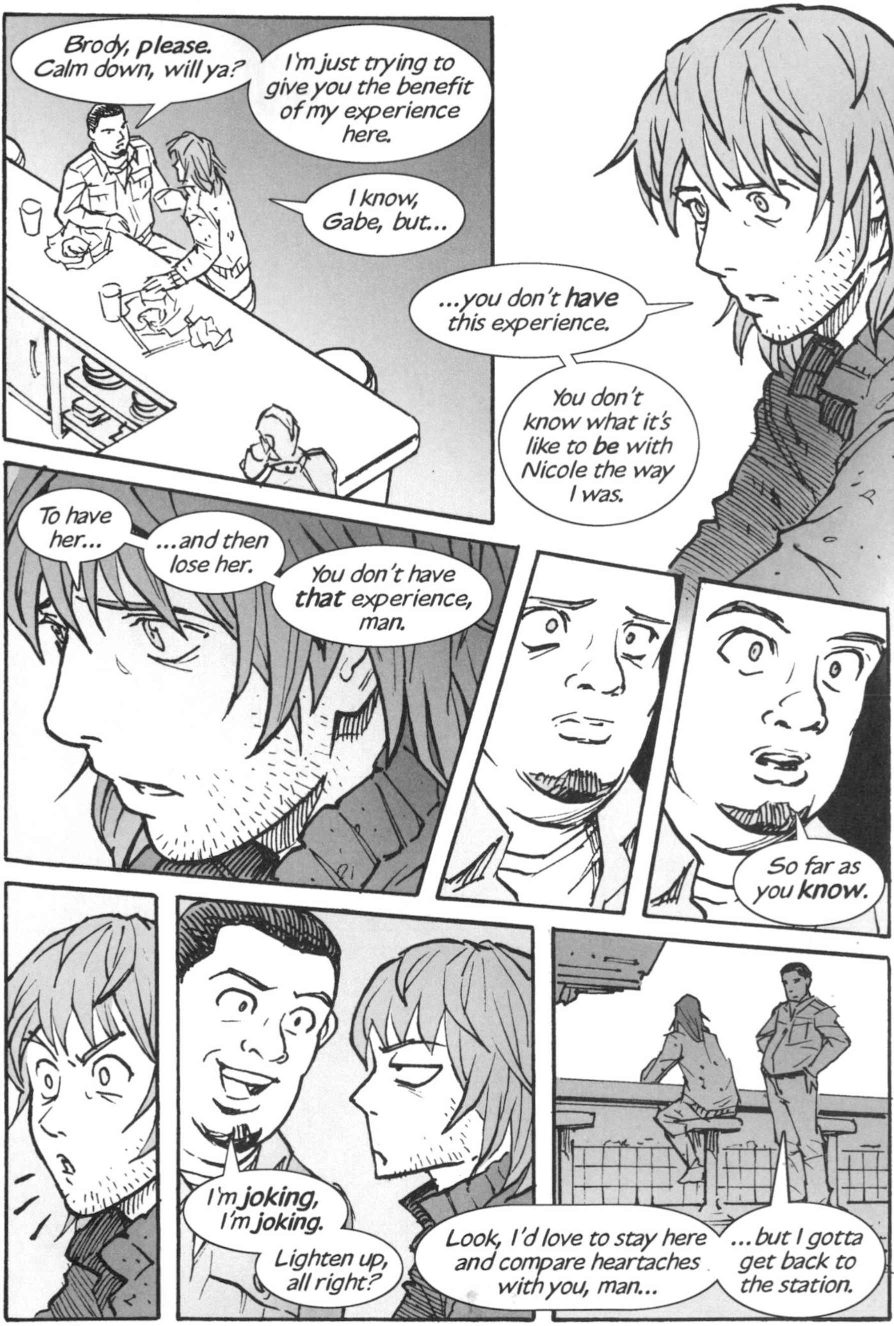
Brody, please. Calm down, will ya?
I'm just trying to give you the benefit of my experience here.
I know, Gabe, but...
...you don't have this experience.
You don't know what it's like to be with Nicole the way I was.
To have her...
...and then lose her.
You don't have that experience, man.
So far as you know.
I'm joking, I'm joking.
Lighten up, all right?
Look, I'd love to stay here and compare heartaches with you, man...
...but I gotta get back to the station.

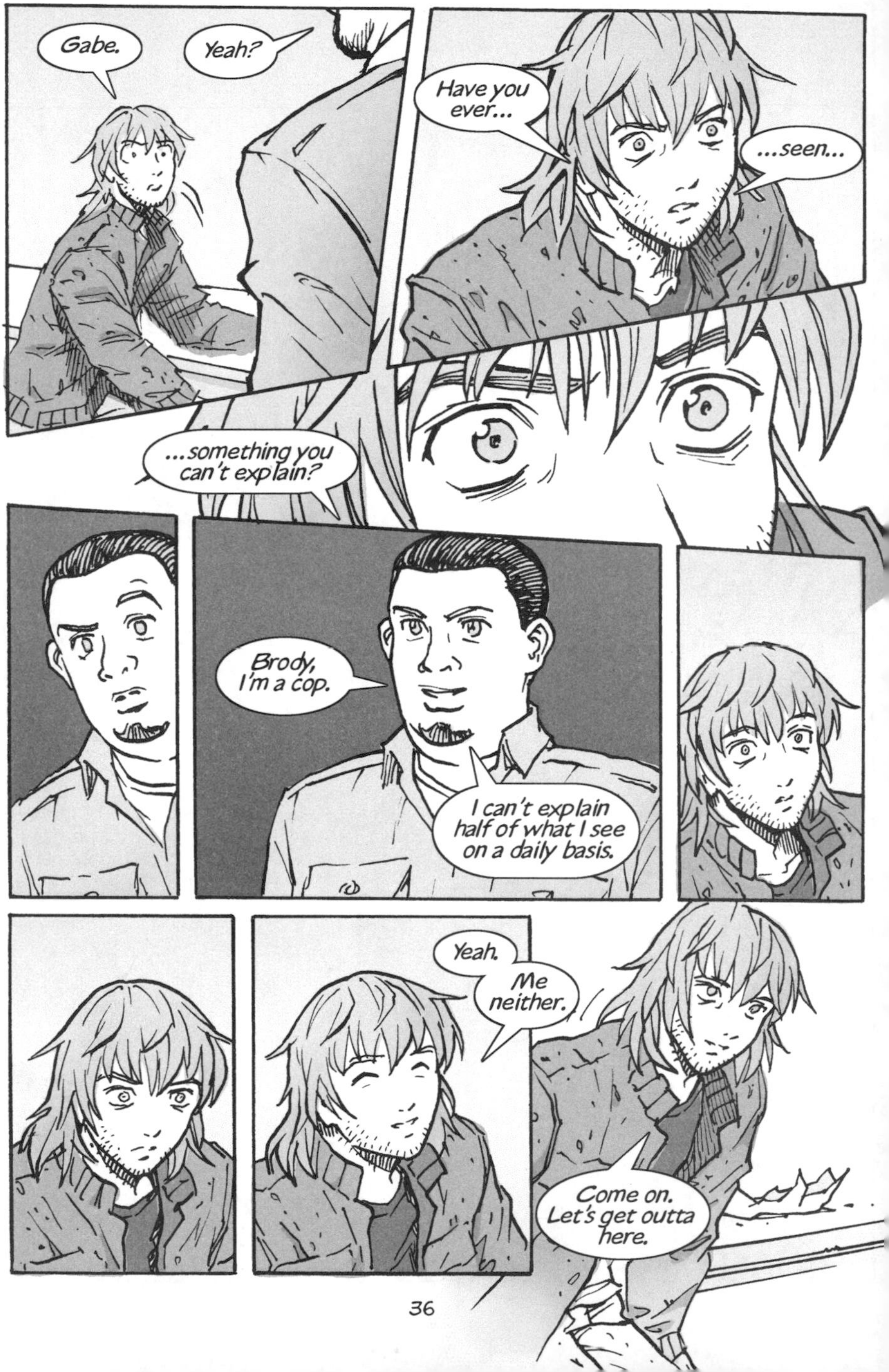
Gabe.
Yeah?
Have you ever...
...seen...
...something you can't explain?
Brody, I'm a cop.
I can't explain half of what I see on a daily basis.
Yeah.
Me neither.
Come on. Let's get outta here.

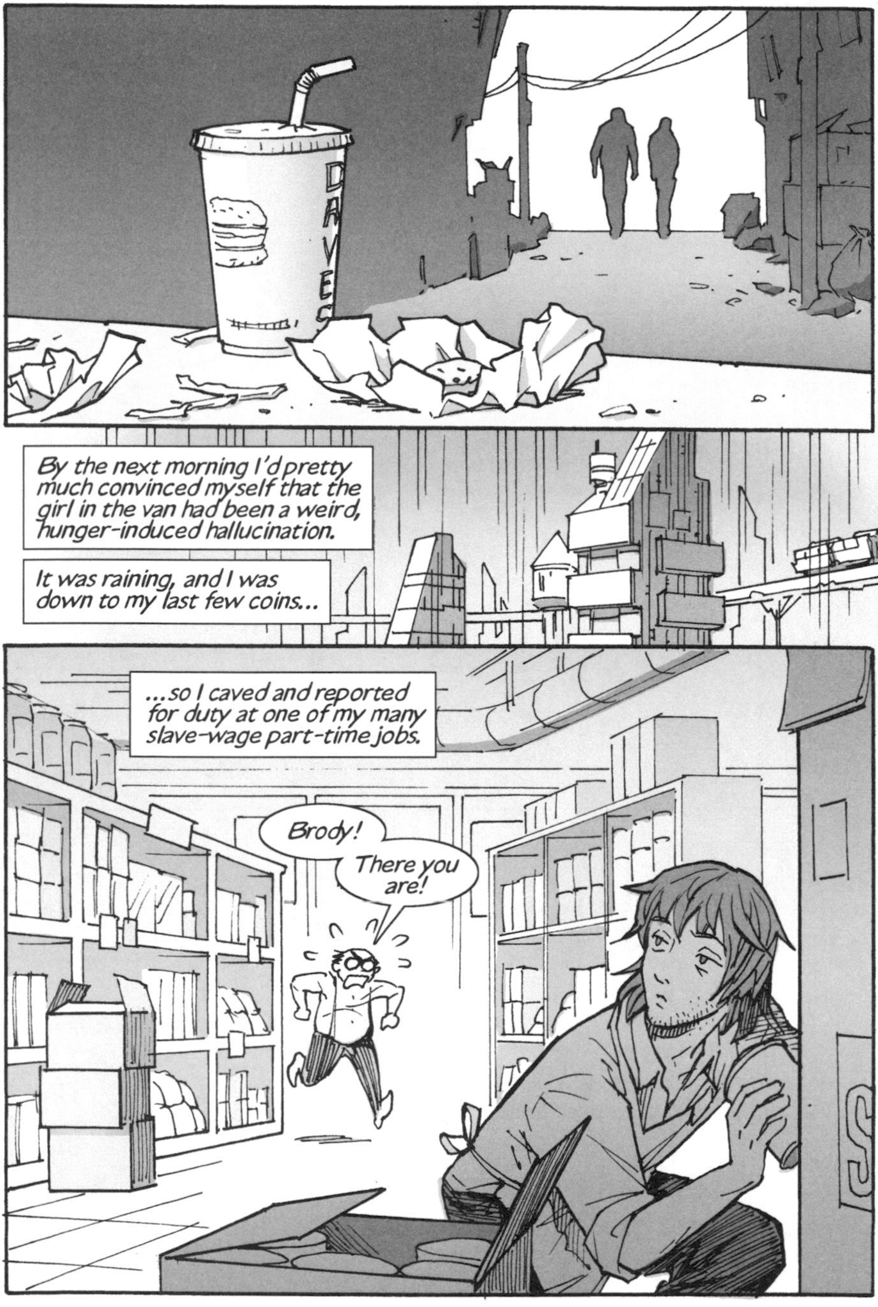
By the next morning I'd pretty much convinced myself that the girl in the van had been a weird, hunger-induced hallucination.
It was raining, and I was down to my last few coins...
...so I caved and reported for duty at one of my many slave-wage part-time jobs.
Brody!
There you are!

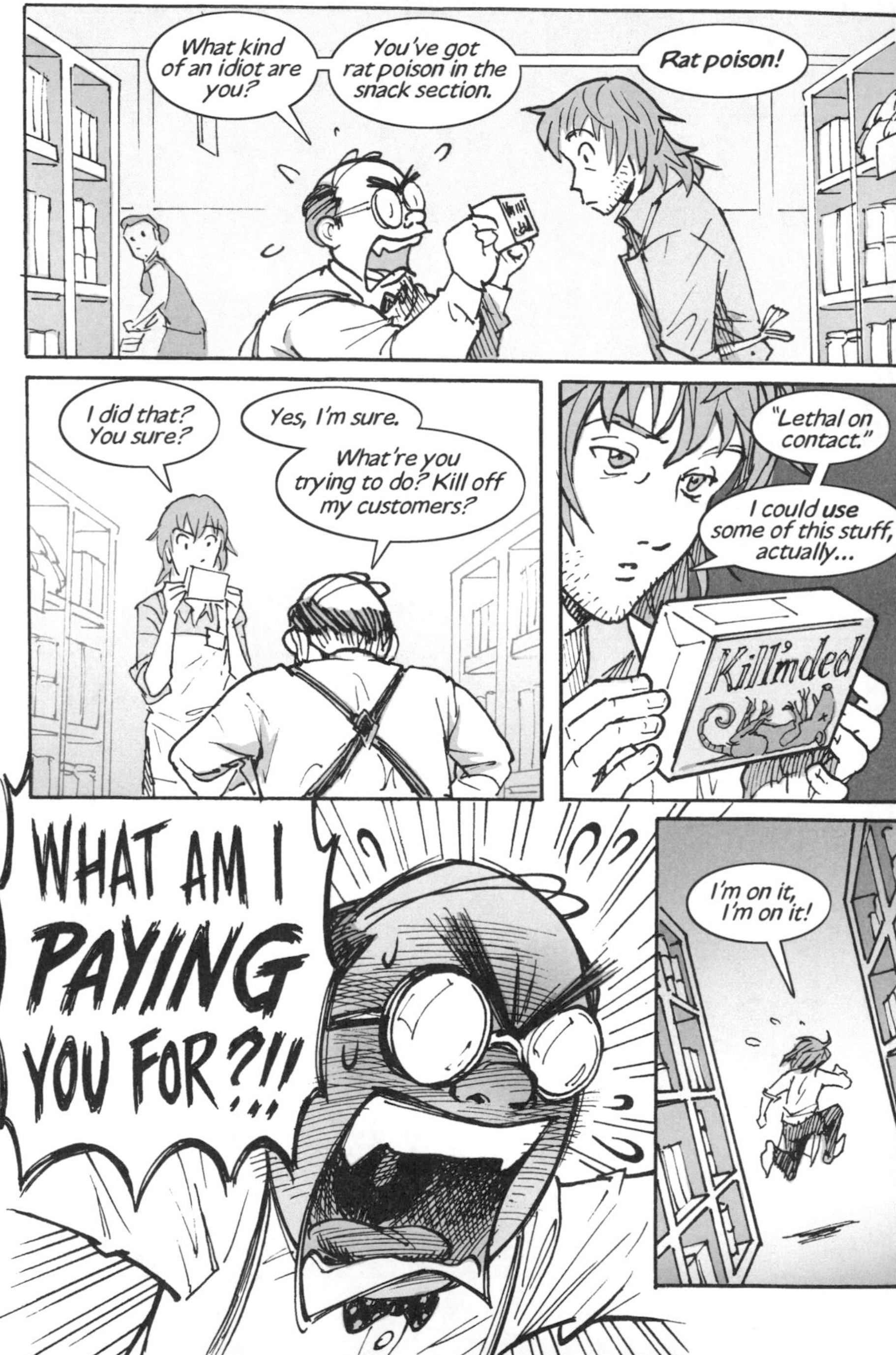
What kind of an idiot are you?
You've got rat poison in the snack section.
Rat poison!
I did that? You sure?
Yes, I'm sure.
What're you trying to do? Kill off my customers?
"Lethal on contact."
I could use some of this stuff, actually...
Kill'mded
WHAT AM I PAYING YOU FOR?!!
I'm on it, I'm on it!

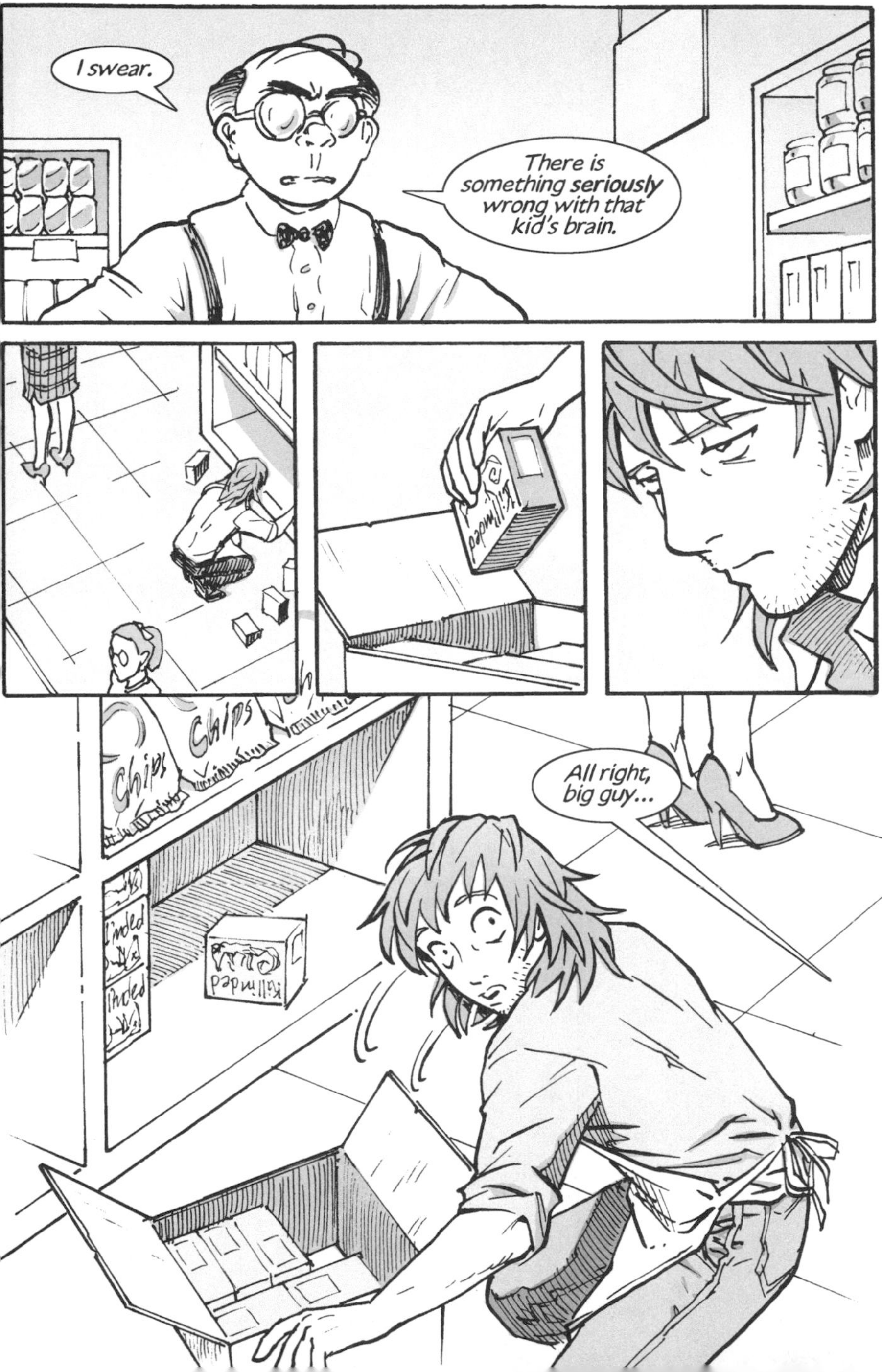
I swear.
There is something seriously wrong with that kid's brain.
Chips
All right, big guy...

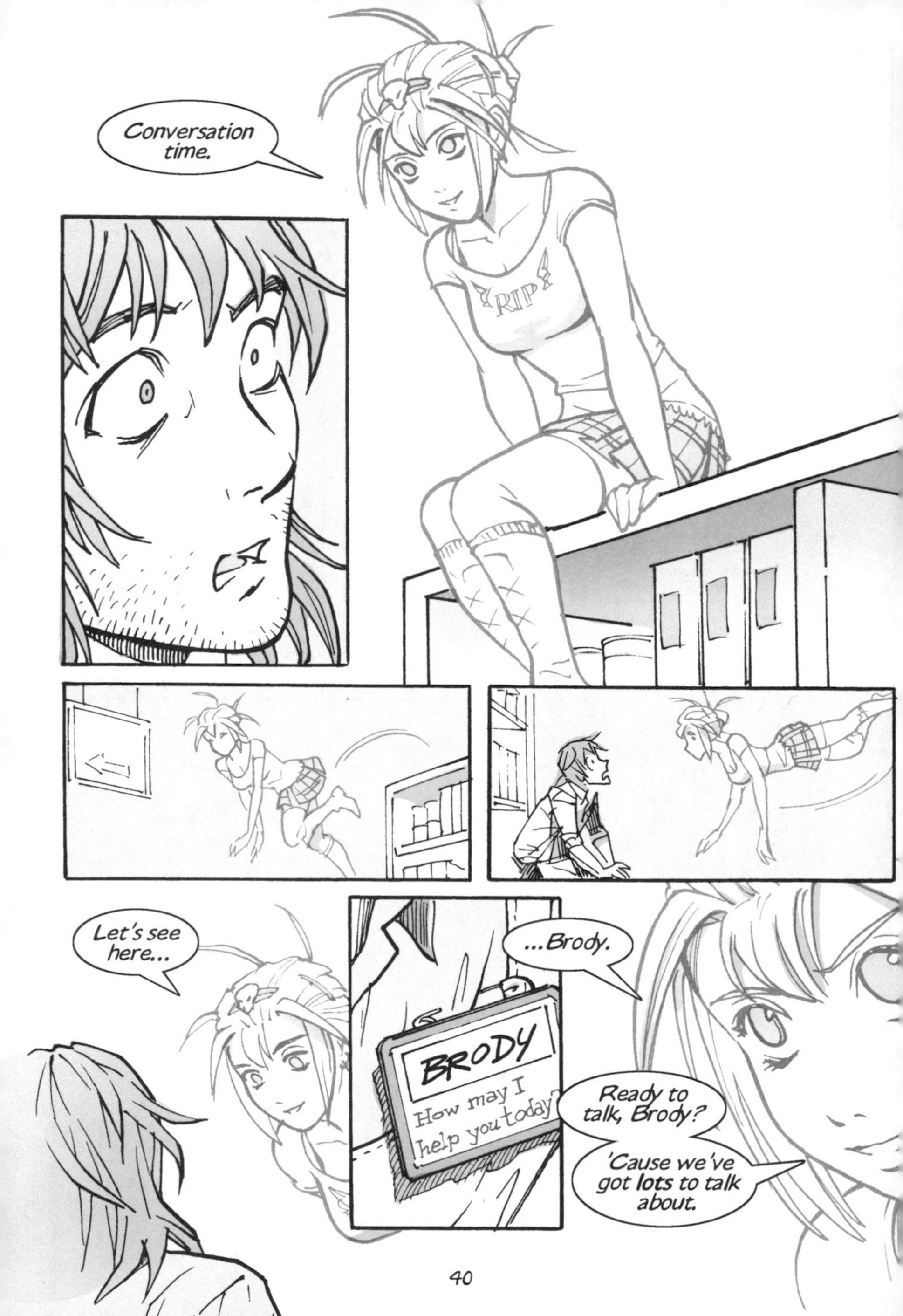
Conversation time.
RIP
Let's see here...
...Brody.
BRODY
How may I help you today?
Ready to talk, Brody?
'Cause we've got **lots** to talk about.

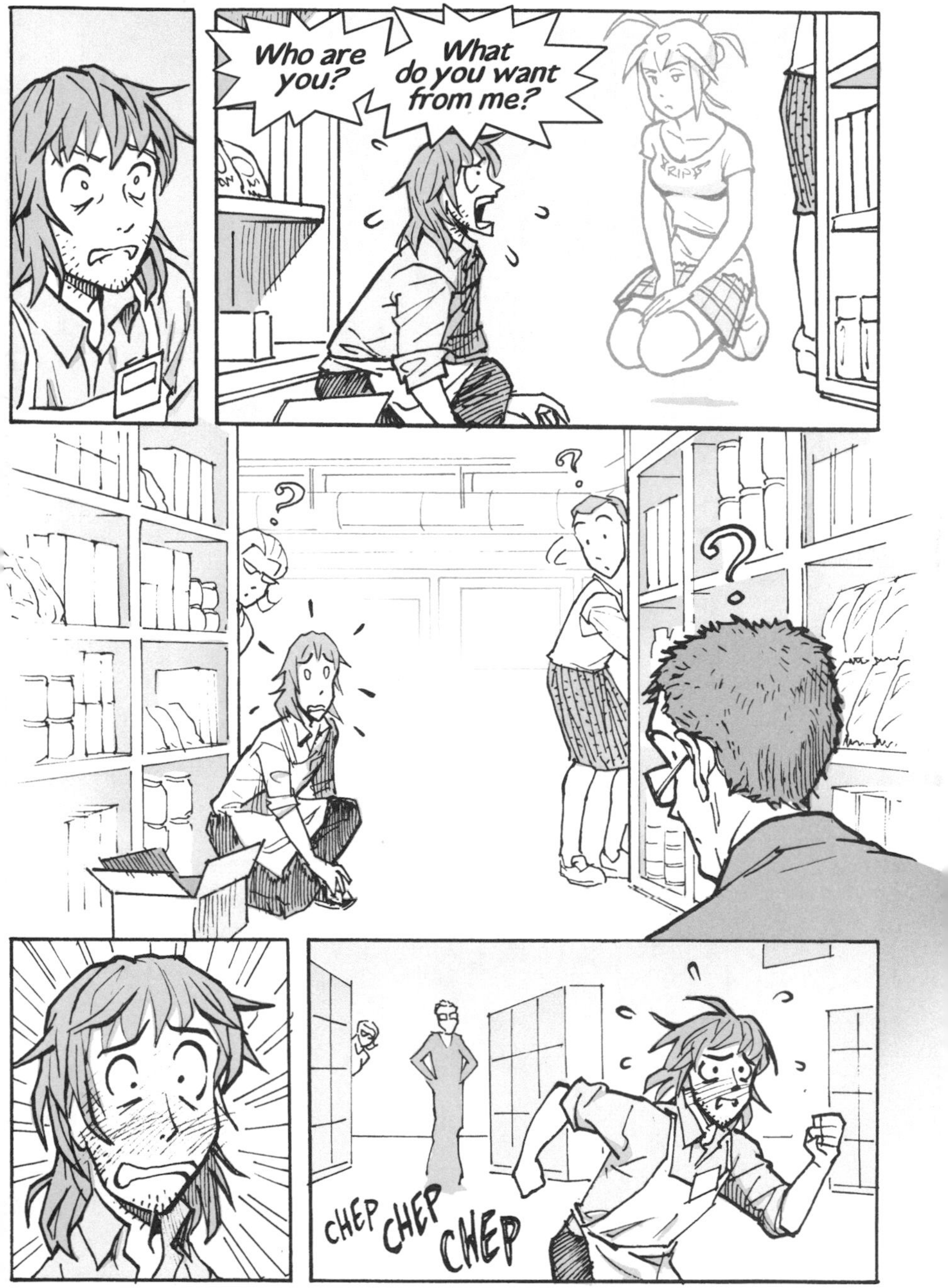
Who are you?
What do you want from me?
CHEP CHEP CHEP

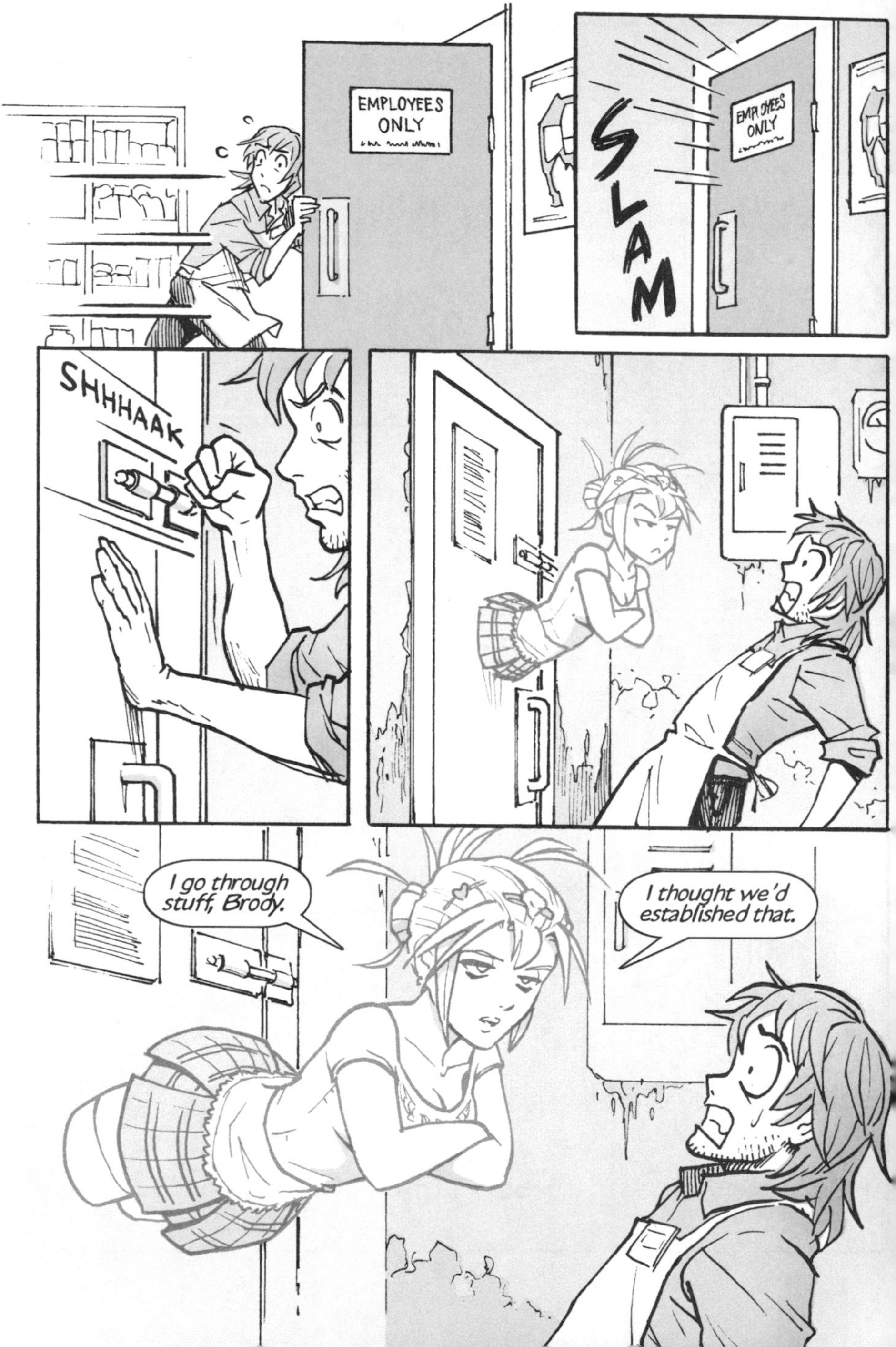
EMPLOYEES ONLY
EMPLOYEES ONLY
SLAM
SHHHAAK
I go through stuff, Brody.
I thought we'd established that.

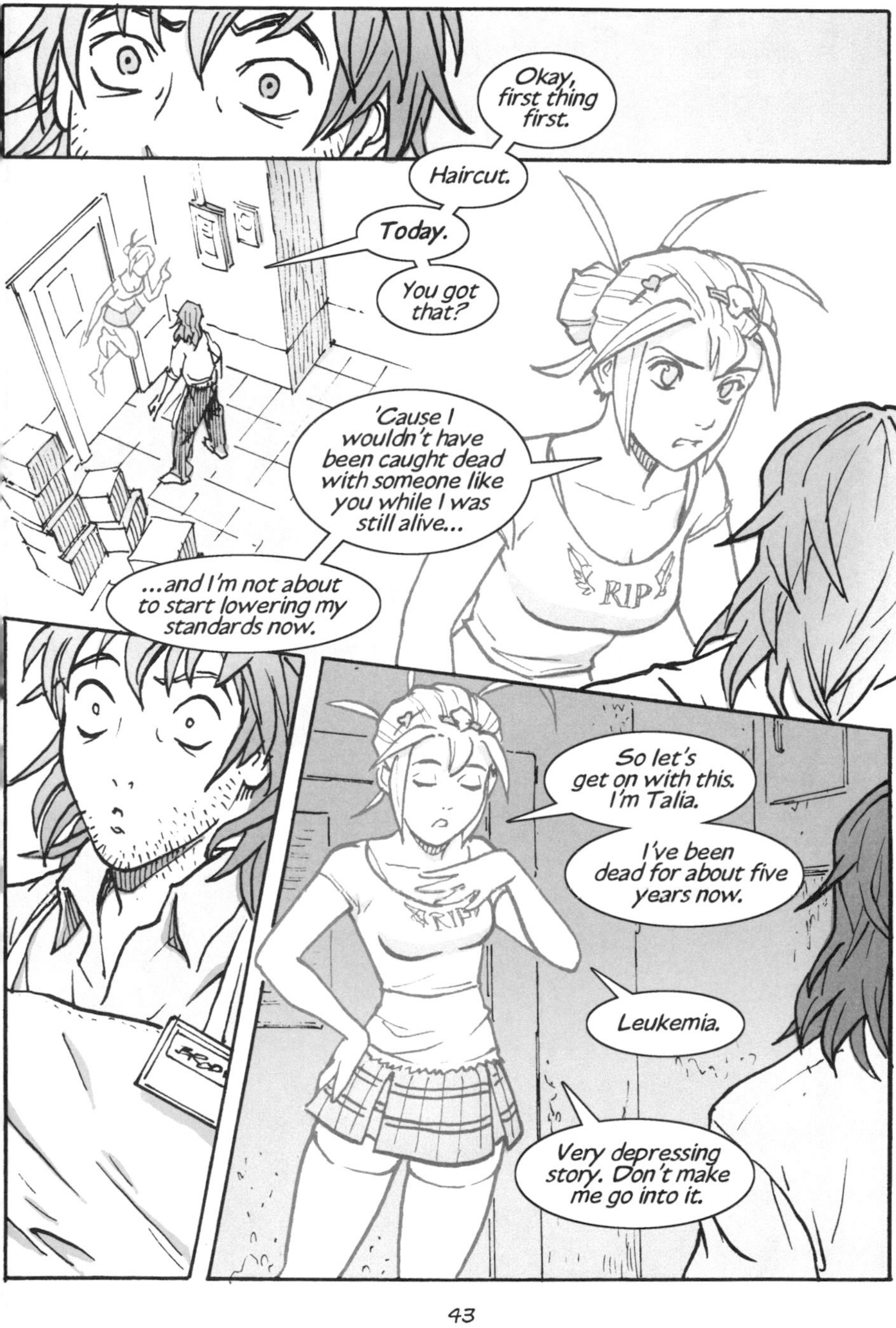
Okay, first thing first.
Haircut.
Today.
You got that?
'Cause I wouldn't have been caught dead with someone like you while I was still alive...
...and I'm not about to start lowering my standards now.
RIP
So let's get on with this. I'm Talia.
I've been dead for about five years now.
Leukemia.
Very depressing story. Don't make me go into it.

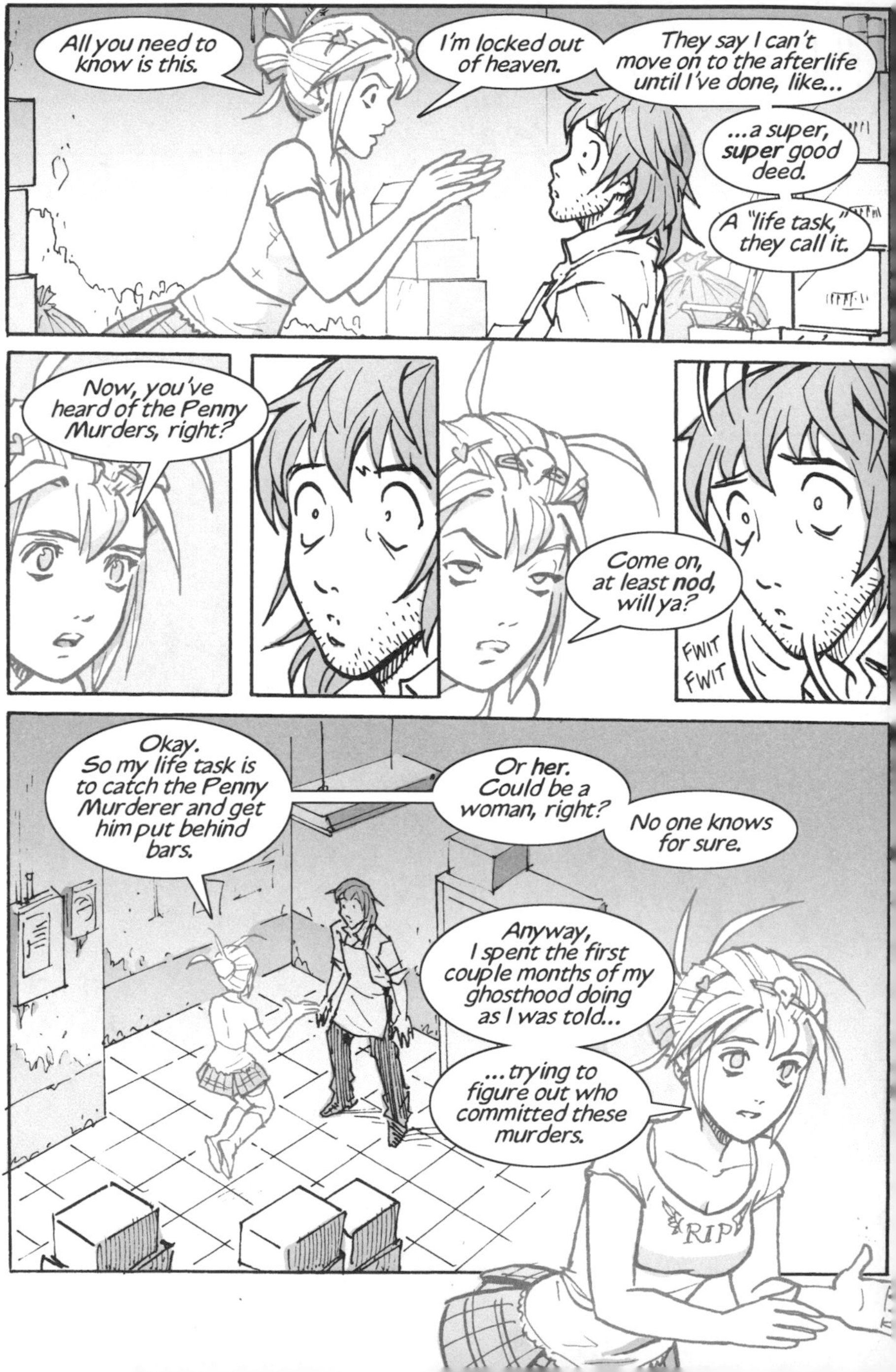
All you need to know is this.
I'm locked out of heaven.
They say I can't move on to the afterlife until I've done, like...
...a super, super good deed.
A "life task," they call it.
Now, you've heard of the Penny Murders, right?
Come on, at least nod, will ya?
FWIT FWIT
Okay. So my life task is to catch the Penny Murderer and get him put behind bars.
Or her. Could be a woman, right?
No one knows for sure.
Anyway, I spent the first couple months of my ghosthood doing as I was told...
...trying to figure out who committed these murders.
RIP

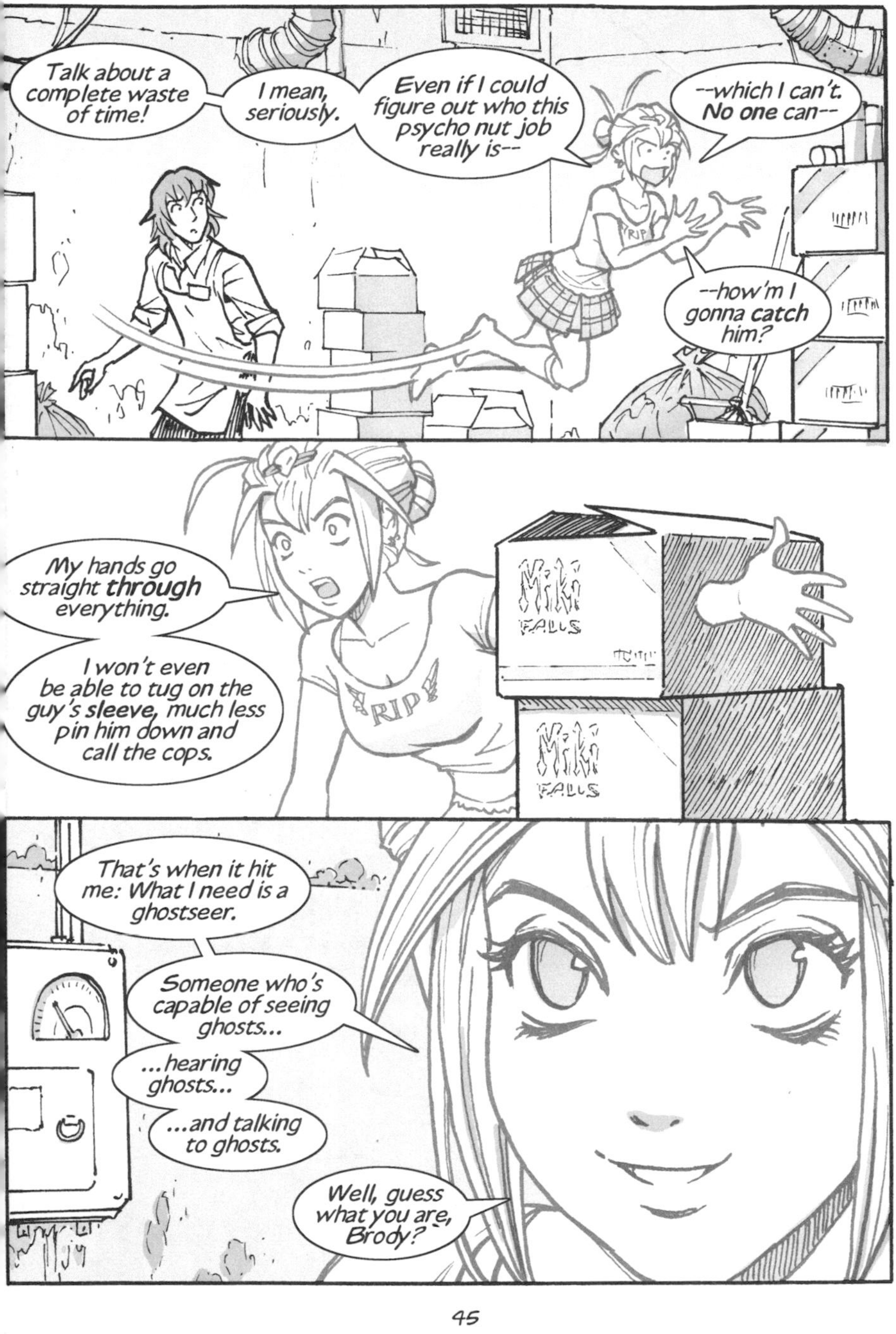
Talk about a complete waste of time!
I mean, seriously.
Even if I could figure out who this psycho nut job really is--
--which I can't. No one can--
--how'm I gonna catch him?
My hands go straight through everything.
I won't even be able to tug on the guy's sleeve, much less pin him down and call the cops.
MIKI FALLS
MIKI FALLS
That's when it hit me: What I need is a ghostseer.
Someone who's capable of seeing ghosts...
...hearing ghosts...
...and talking to ghosts.
Well, guess what you are, Brody?

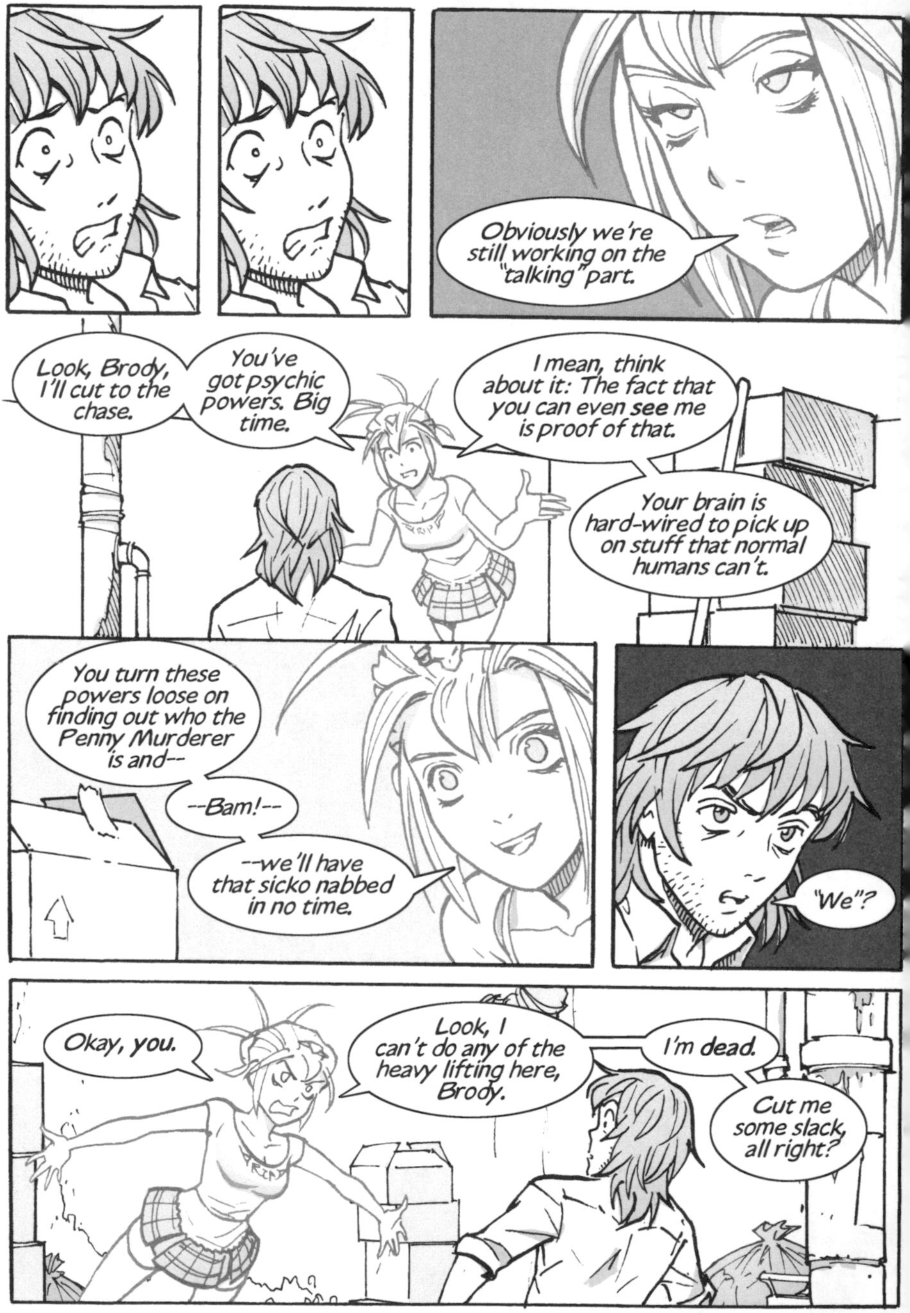
Obviously we're still working on the "talking" part.
Look, Brody, I'll cut to the chase.
You've got psychic powers. Big time.
I mean, think about it: The fact that you can even see me is proof of that.
Your brain is hard-wired to pick up on stuff that normal humans can't.
You turn these powers loose on finding out who the Penny Murderer is and--
--Bam!--
--we'll have that sicko nabbed in no time.
"We"?
Okay, you.
Look, I can't do any of the heavy lifting here, Brody.
I'm dead.
Cut me some slack, all right?

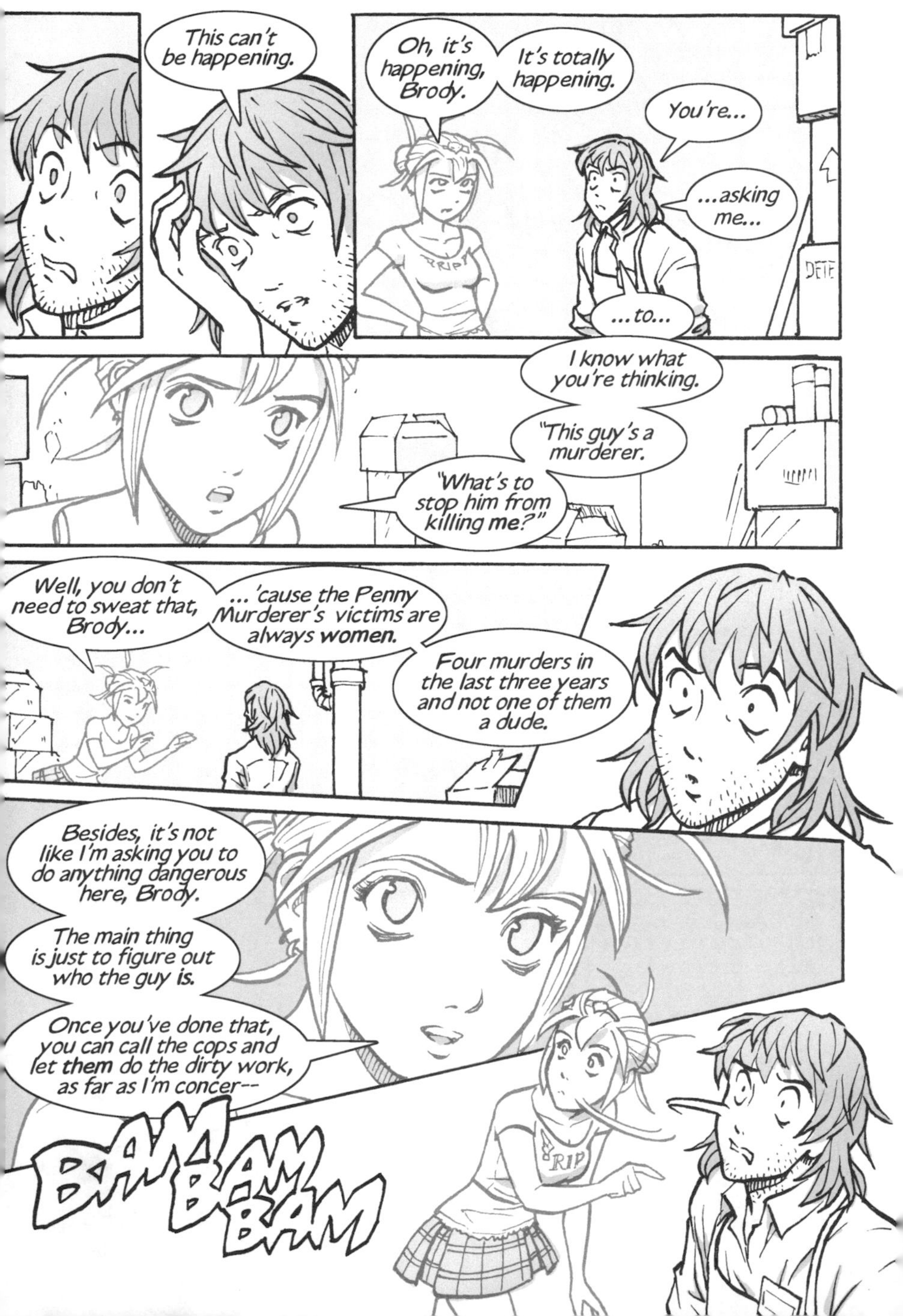

This can't be happening.
Oh, it's happening, Brody.
It's totally happening.
You're...
...asking me...
...to...
RIP
DETE
I know what you're thinking.
"This guy's a murderer.
"What's to stop him from killing me?"
Well, you don't need to sweat that, Brody...
...'cause the Penny Murderer's victims are always **women**.
Four murders in the last three years and not one of them a dude.
Besides, it's not like I'm asking you to do anything dangerous here, Brody.
The main thing is just to figure out who the guy **is**.
Once you've done that, you can call the cops and let **them** do the dirty work, as far as I'm concer--
BAM BAM BAM
RIP

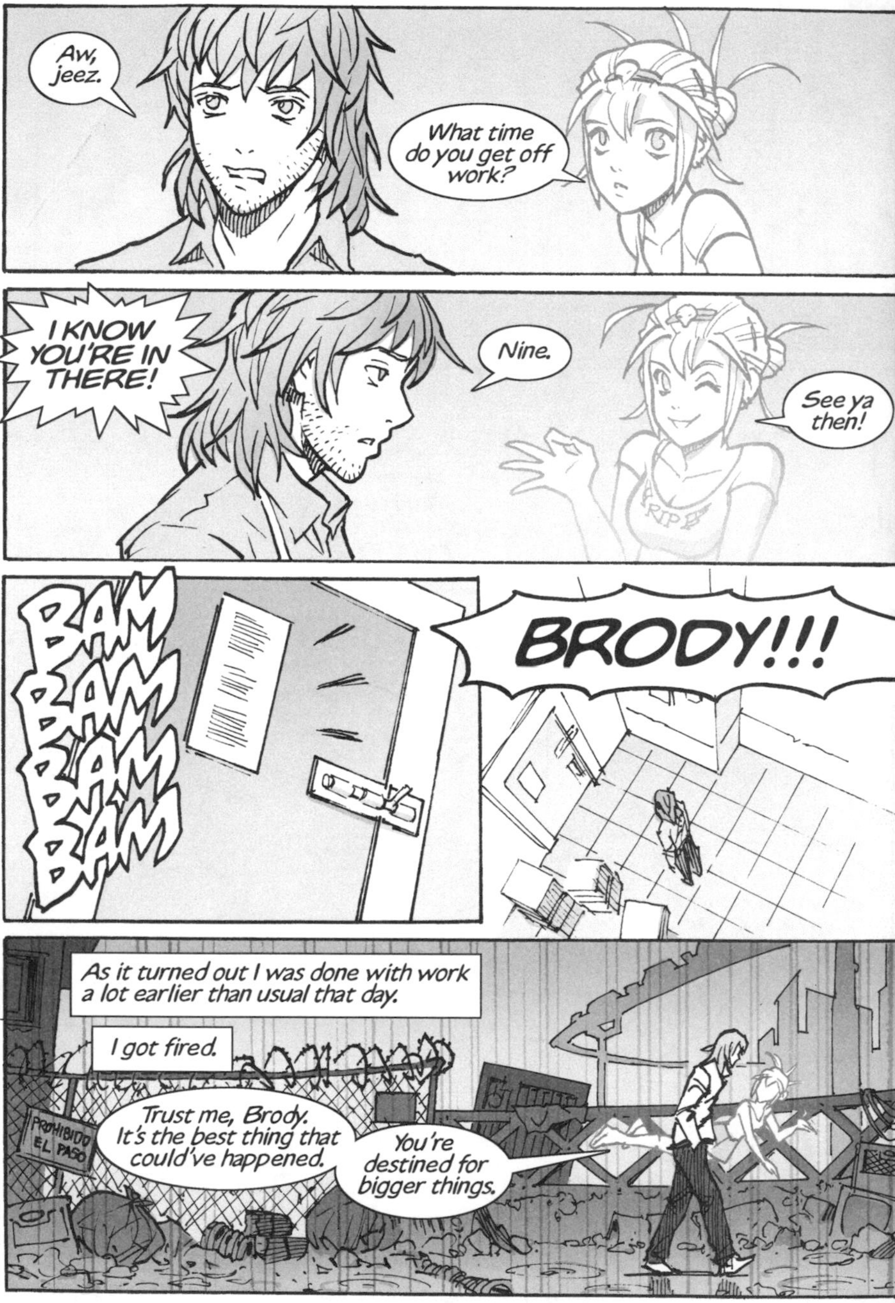
Aw, jeez.
What time do you get off work?
I KNOW YOU'RE IN THERE!
Nine.
See ya then!
BAM BAM BAM BAM
BRODY!!!
As it turned out I was done with work a lot earlier than usual that day.
I got fired.
PROHIBIDO EL PASO
Trust me, Brody. It's the best thing that could've happened.
You're destined for bigger things.

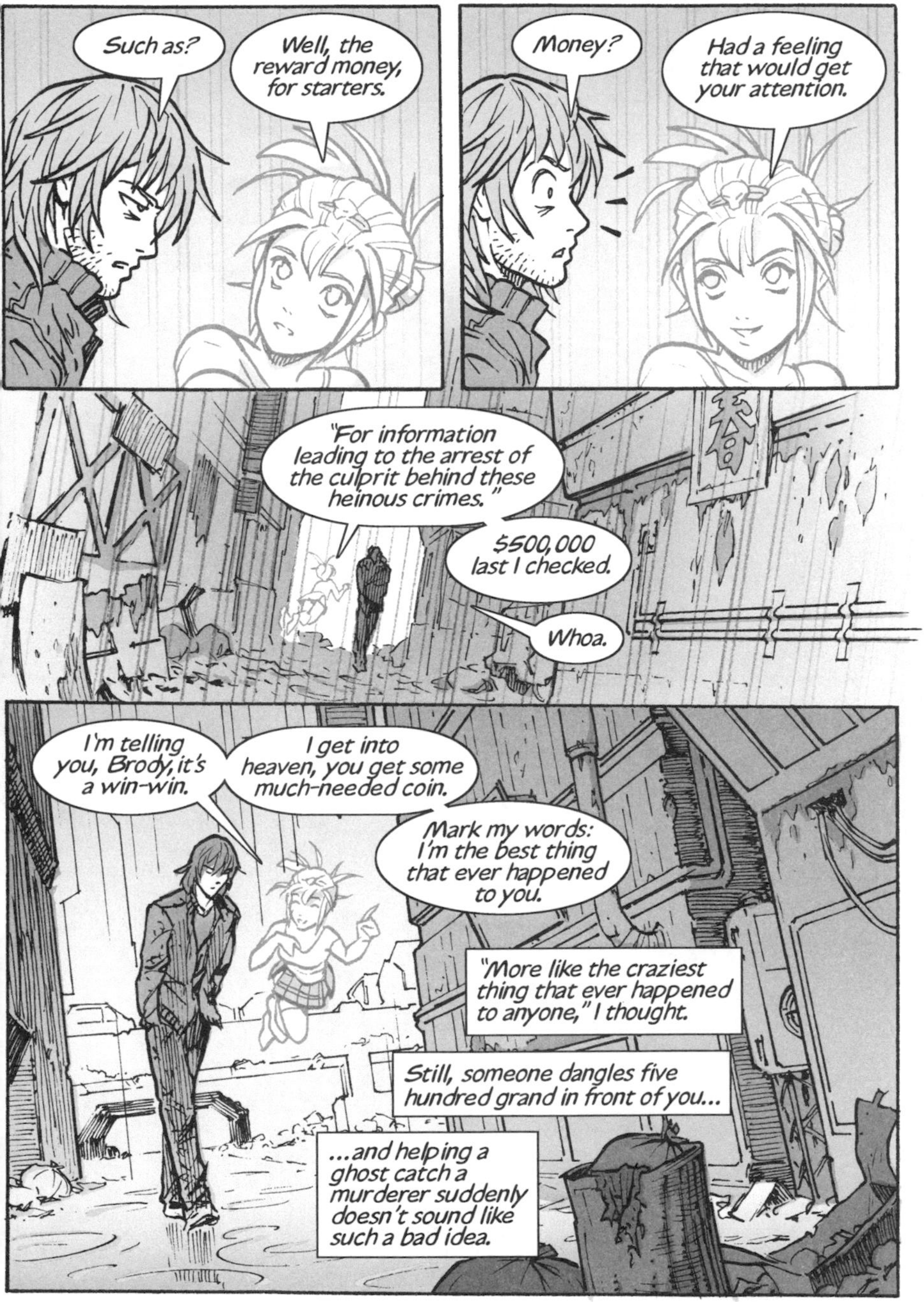
Such as?
Well, the reward money, for starters.
Money?
Had a feeling that would get your attention.
"For information leading to the arrest of the culprit behind these heinous crimes."
$500,000 last I checked.
Whoa.
I'm telling you, Brody, it's a win-win.
I get into heaven, you get some much-needed coin.
Mark my words: I'm the best thing that ever happened to you.
"More like the craziest thing that ever happened to anyone," I thought.
Still, someone dangles five hundred grand in front of you...
...and helping a ghost catch a murderer suddenly doesn't sound like such a bad idea.

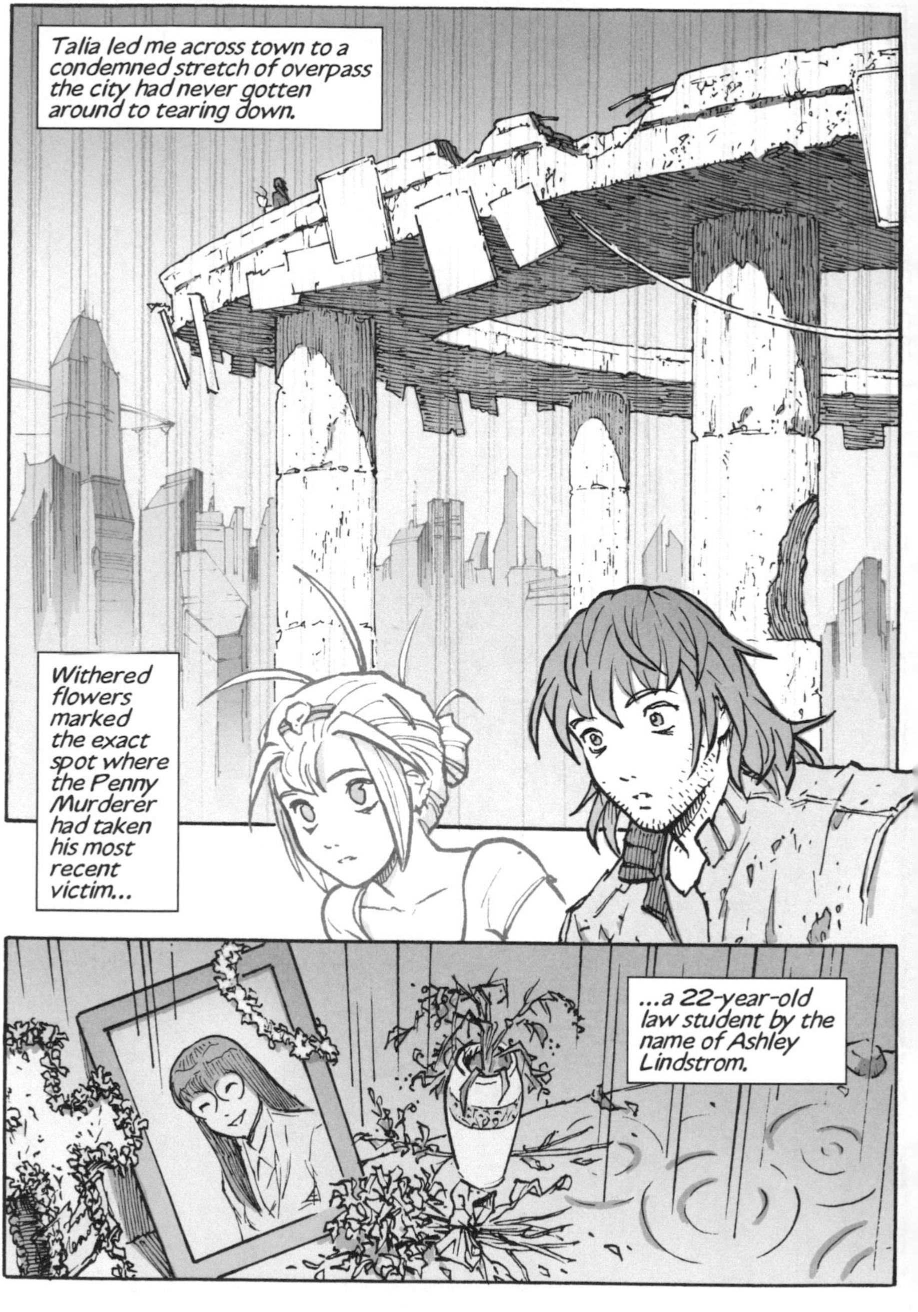
Talia led me across town to a condemned stretch of overpass the city had never gotten around to tearing down.
Withered flowers marked the exact spot where the Penny Murderer had taken his most recent victim...
...a 22-year-old law student by the name of Ashley Lindstrom.

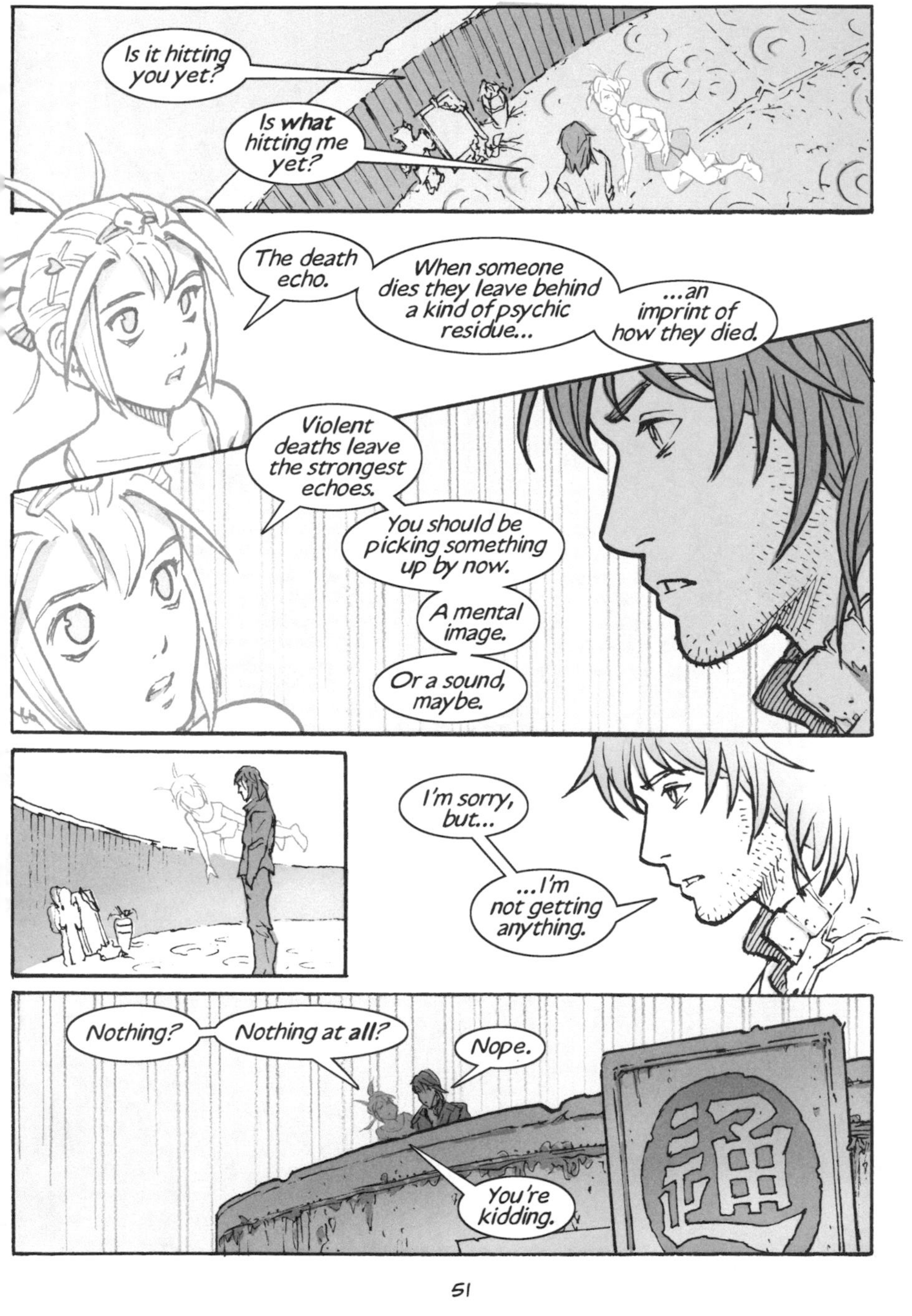

Is it hitting you yet?
Is **what** hitting me yet?
The death echo.
When someone dies they leave behind a kind of psychic residue...
...an imprint of how they died.
Violent deaths leave the strongest echoes.
You should be picking something up by now.
A mental image.
Or a sound, maybe.
I'm sorry, but...
...I'm not getting anything.
Nothing?
Nothing at **all**?
Nope.
You're kidding.

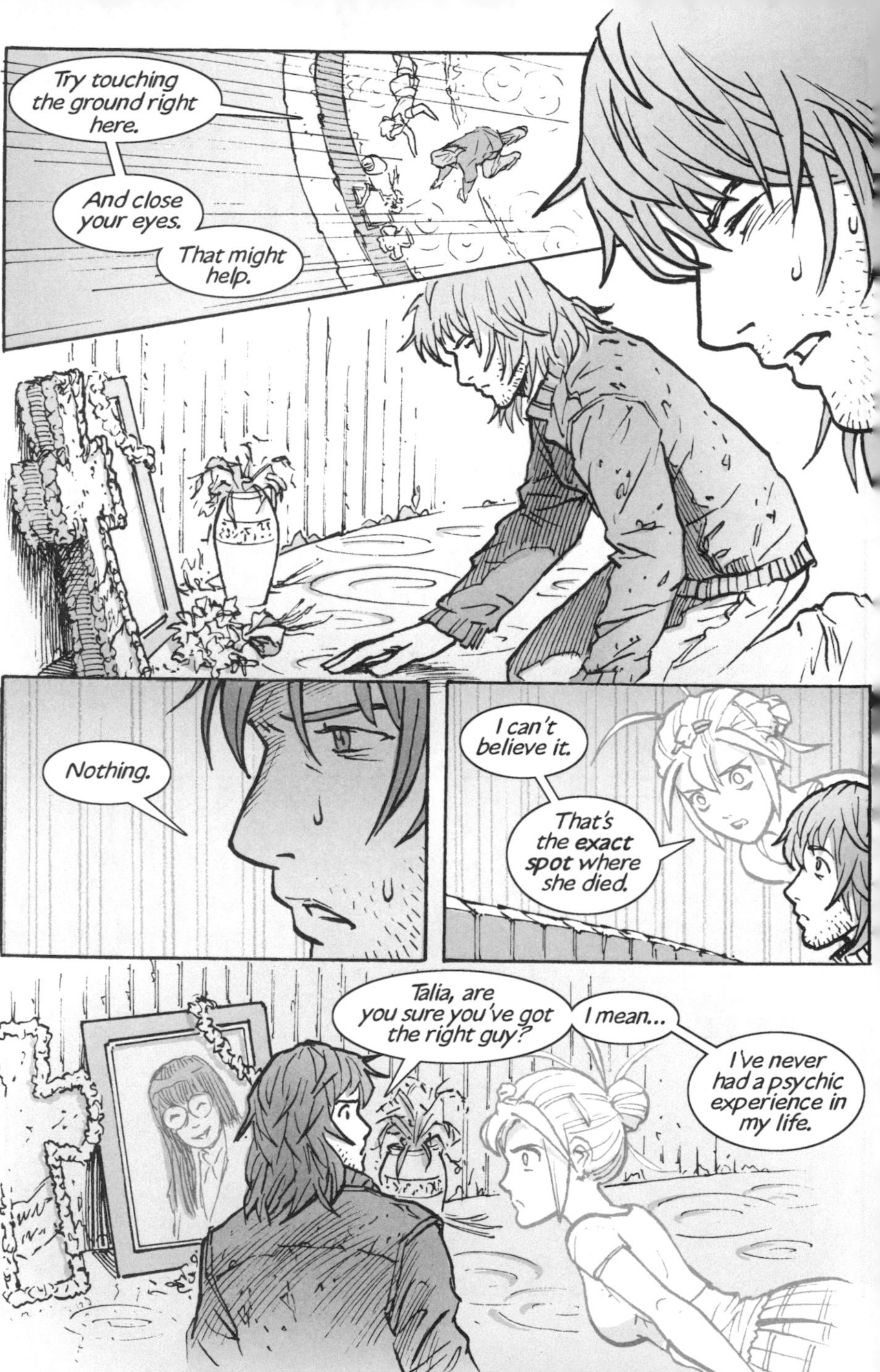
Try touching the ground right here.
And close your eyes.
That might help.
Nothing.
I can't believe it.
That's the **exact spot** where she died.
Talia, are you sure you've got the right guy?
I mean...
I've never had a psychic experience in my life.

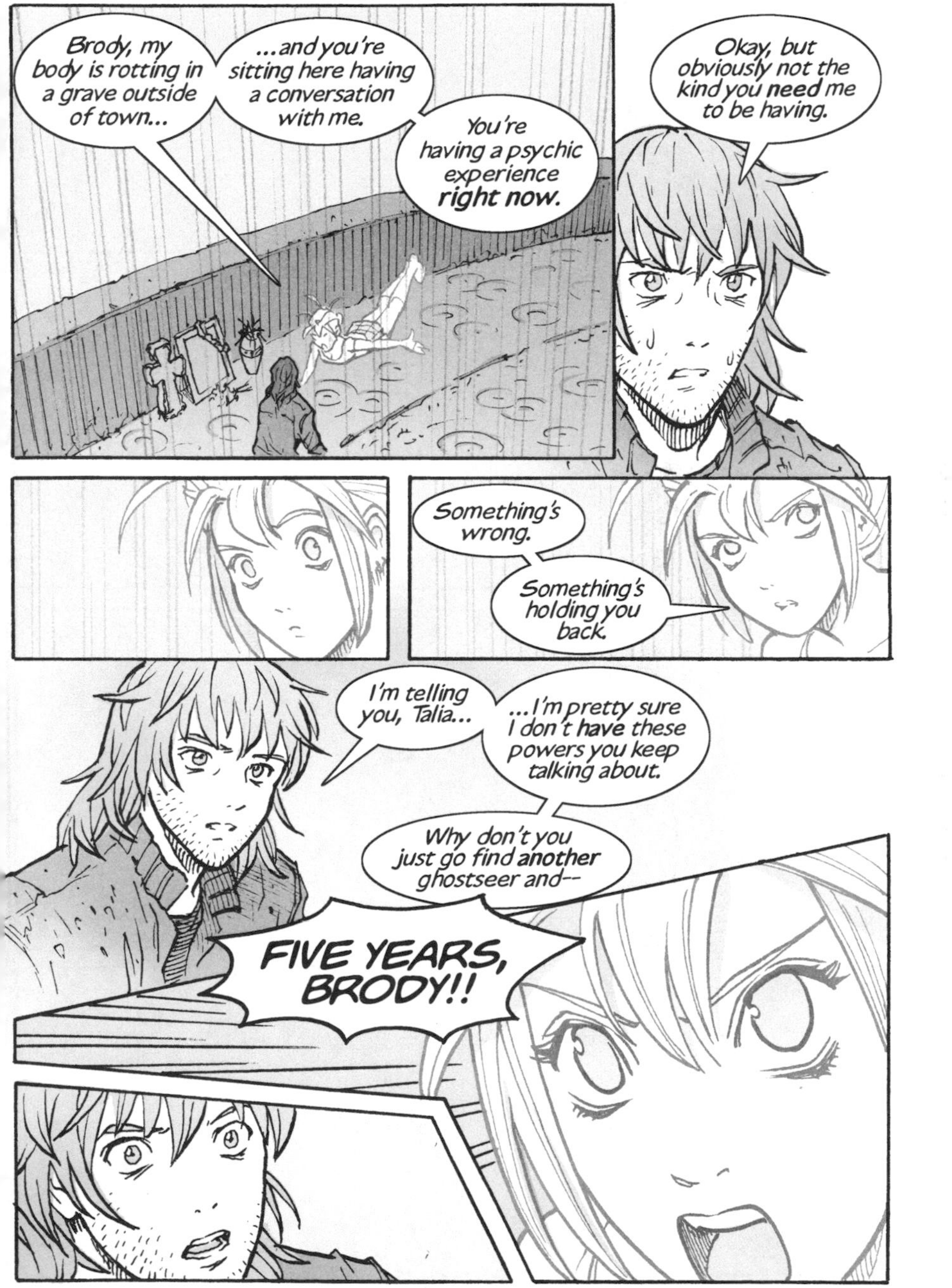
Brody, my body is rotting in a grave outside of town...
...and you're sitting here having a conversation with me.
You're having a psychic experience right now.
Okay, but obviously not the kind you need me to be having.
Something's wrong.
Something's holding you back.
I'm telling you, Talia...
...I'm pretty sure I don't have these powers you keep talking about.
Why don't you just go find another ghostseer and--
FIVE YEARS, BRODY!!

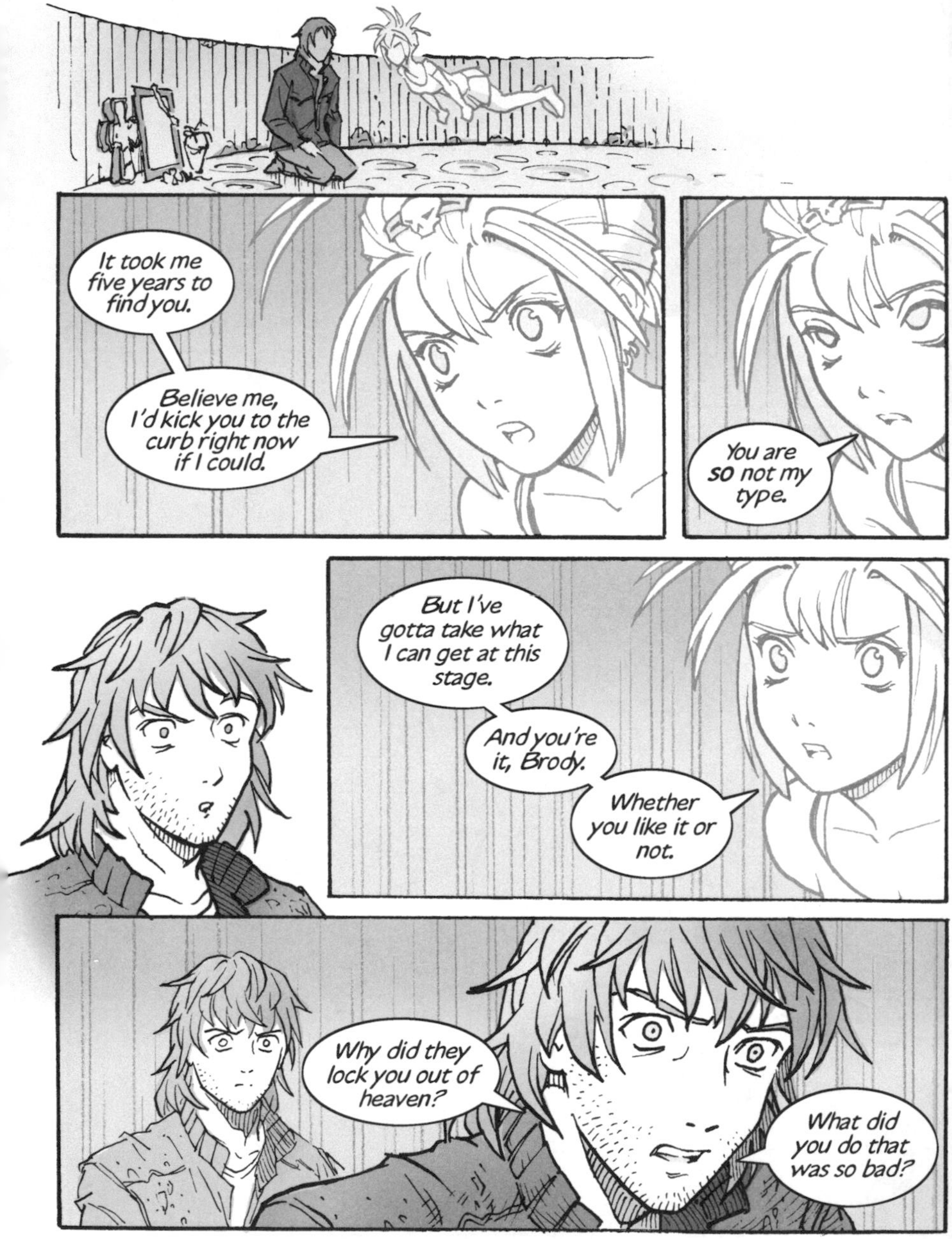
It took me five years to find you.
Believe me, I'd kick you to the curb right now if I could.
You are so not my type.
But I've gotta take what I can get at this stage.
And you're it, Brody.
Whether you like it or not.
Why did they lock you out of heaven?
What did you do that was so bad?

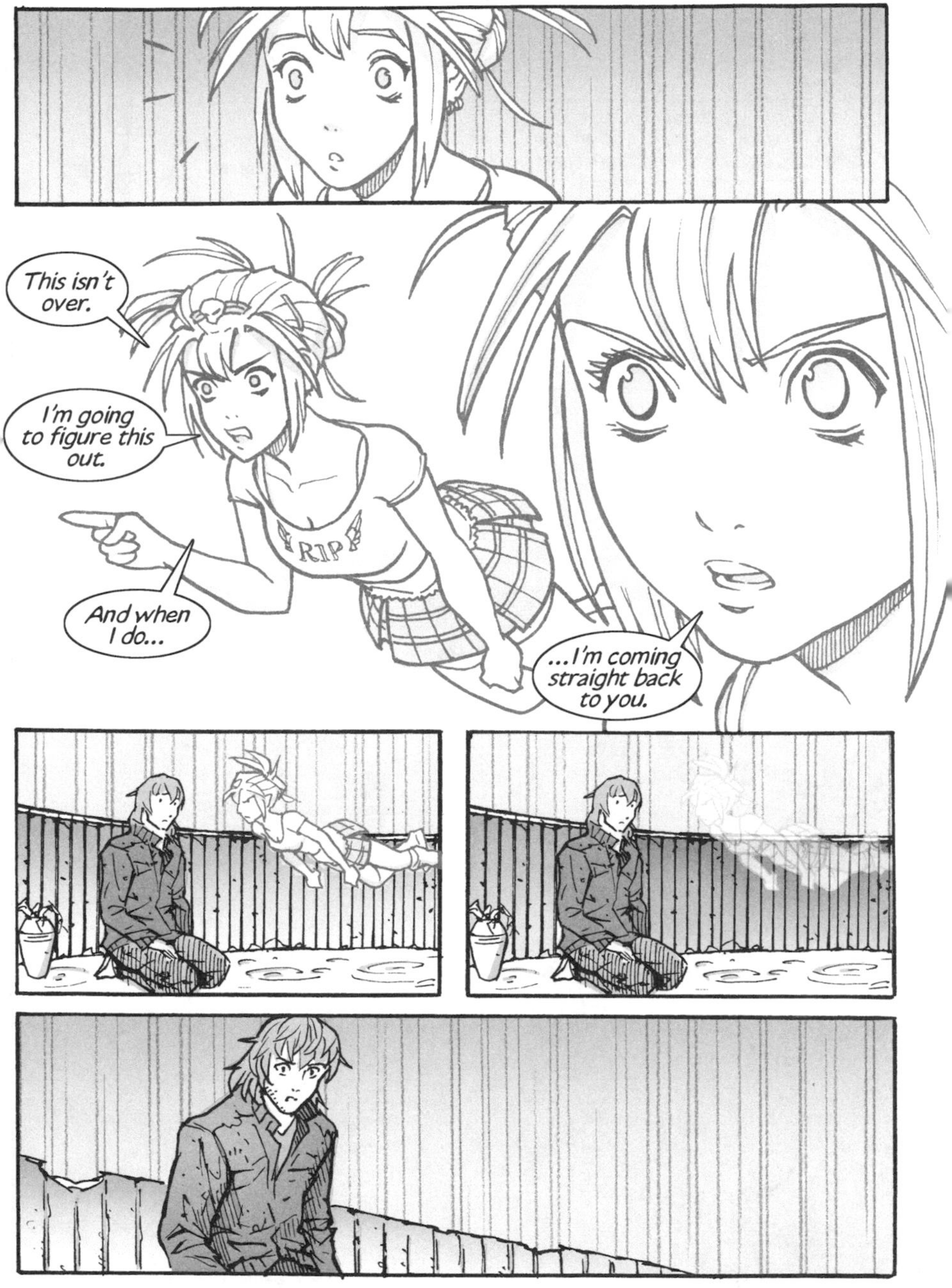

This isn't over.
I'm going to figure this out.
And when I do...
...I'm coming straight back to you.

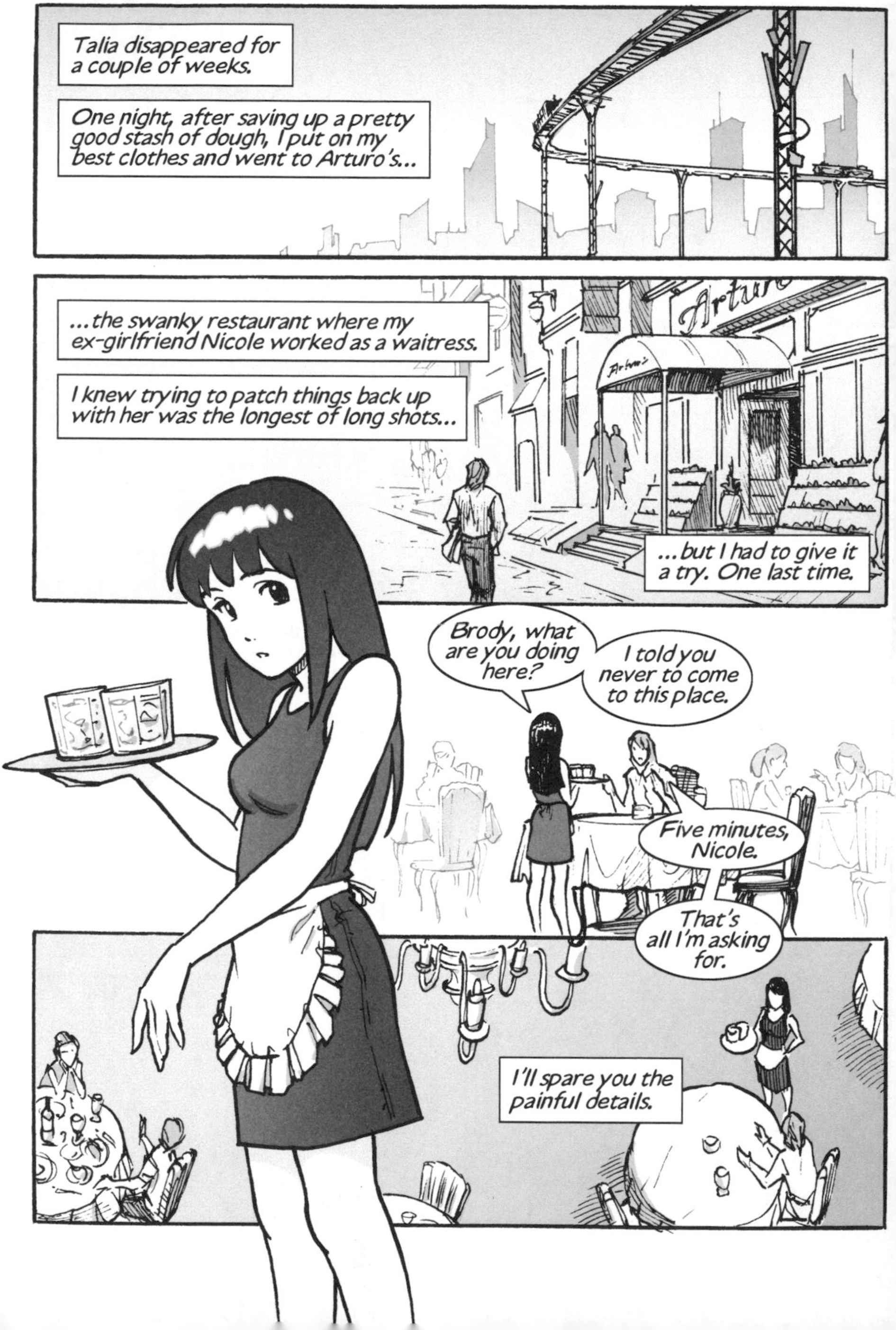
Talia disappeared for a couple of weeks.
One night, after saving up a pretty good stash of dough, I put on my best clothes and went to Arturo's...
...the swanky restaurant where my ex-girlfriend Nicole worked as a waitress.
I knew trying to patch things back up with her was the longest of long shots...
...but I had to give it a try. One last time.
Brody, what are you doing here?
I told you never to come to this place.
Five minutes, Nicole.
That's all I'm asking for.
I'll spare you the painful details.

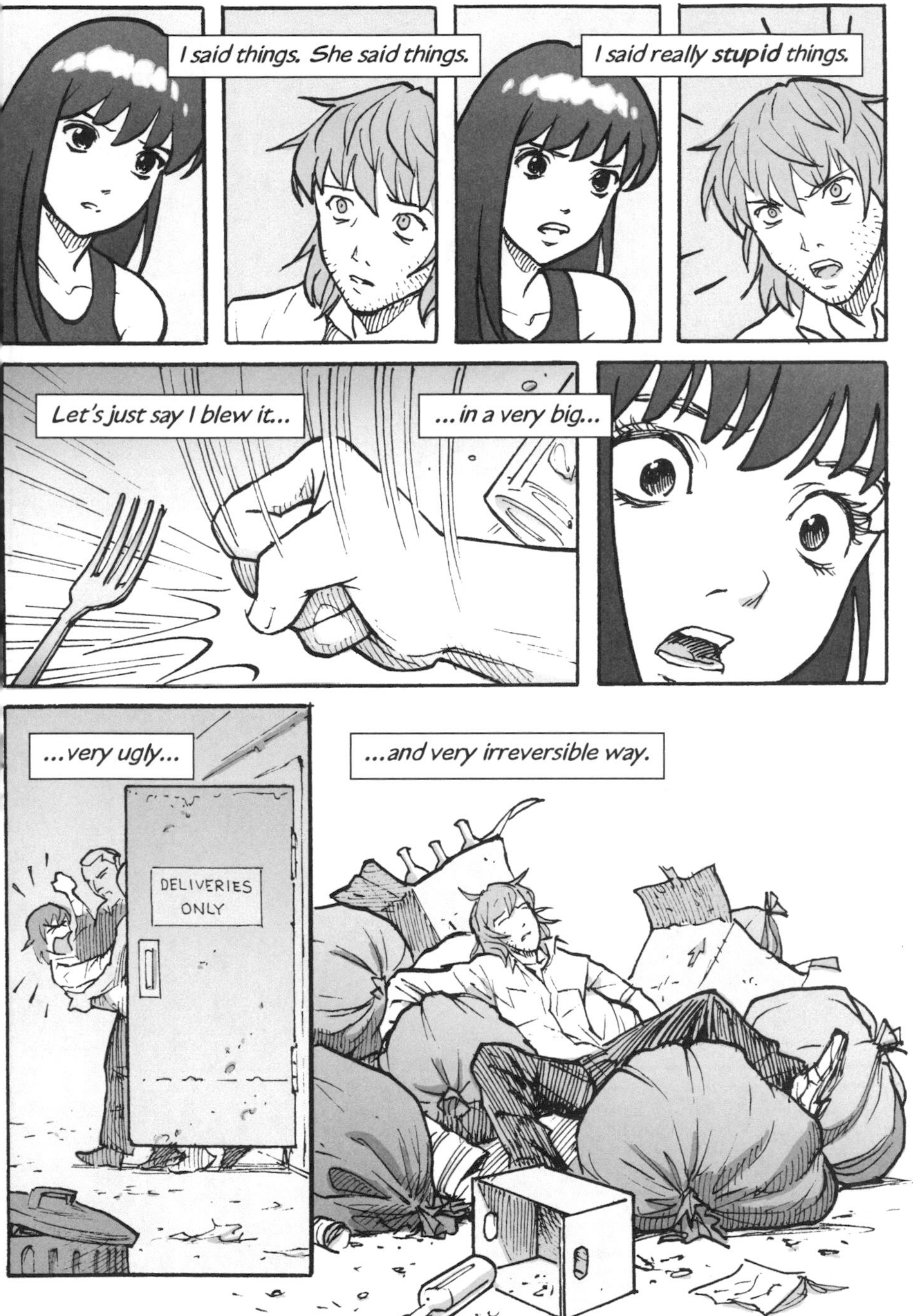

I said things. She said things.
I said really stupid things.
Let's just say I blew it...
...in a very big...
...very ugly...
...and very irreversible way.
DELIVERIES ONLY

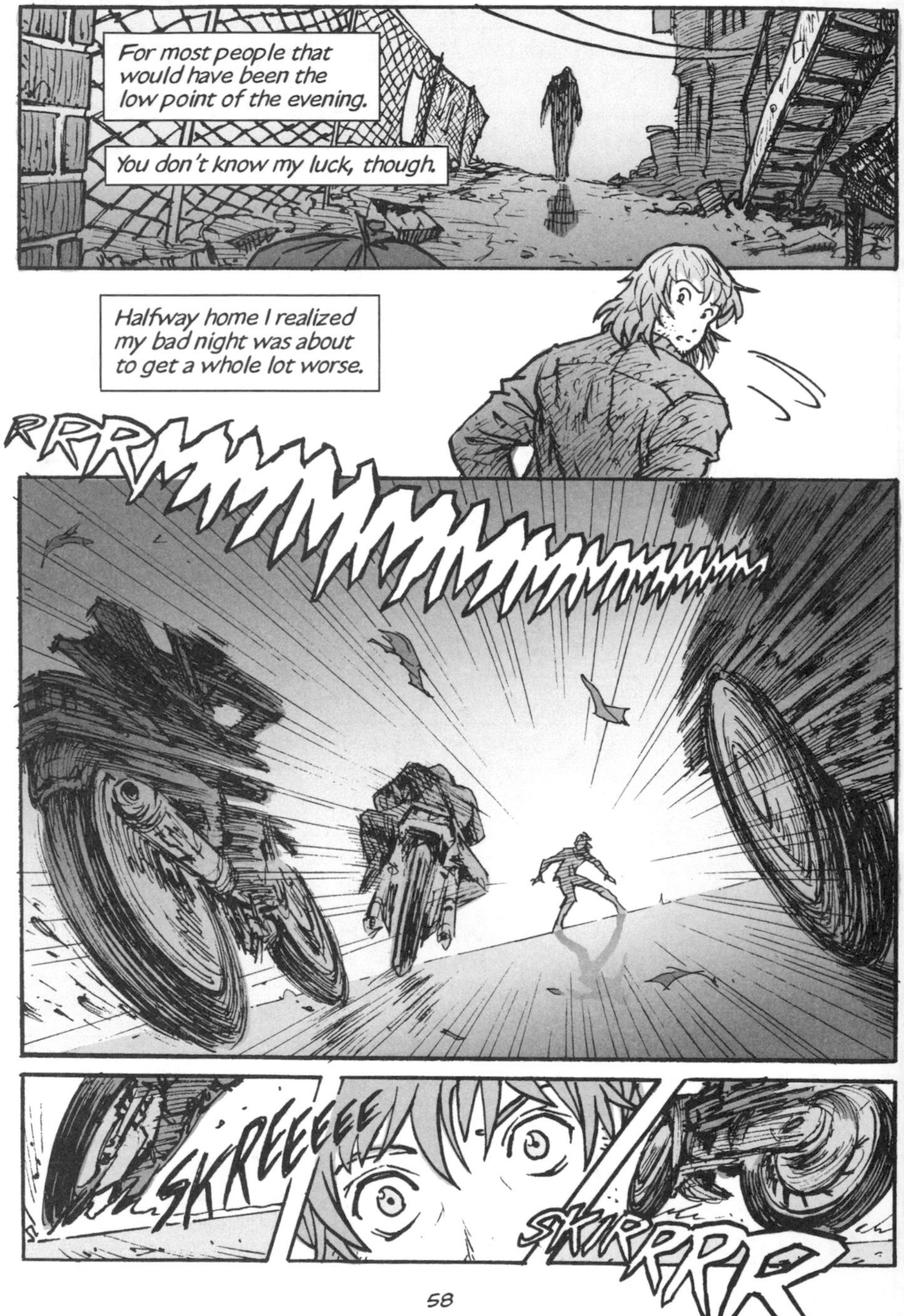
For most people that would have been the low point of the evening.
You don't know my luck, though.
Halfway home I realized my bad night was about to get a whole lot worse.

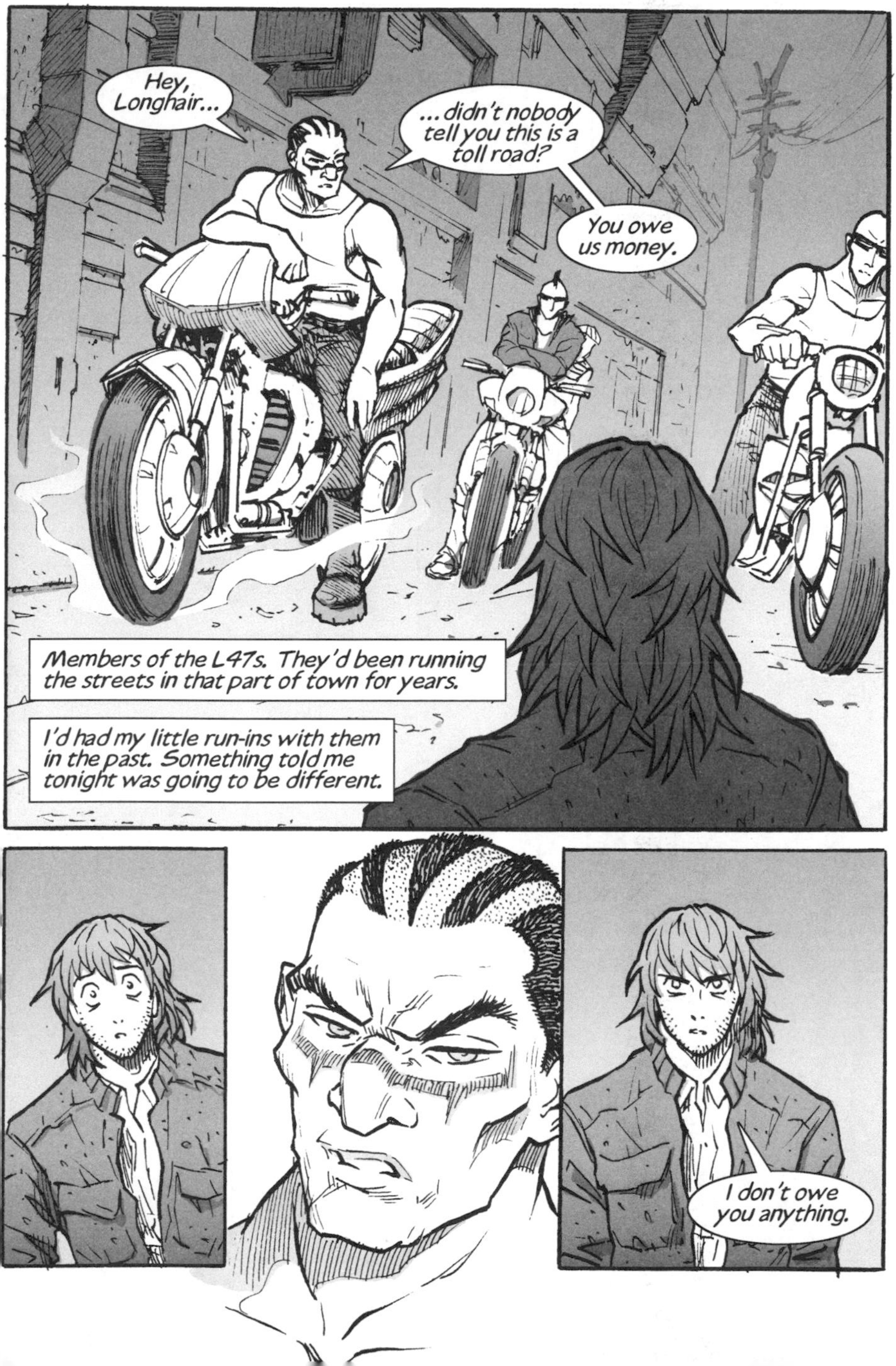
Hey, Longhair...
...didn't nobody tell you this is a toll road?
You owe us money.
Members of the L47s. They'd been running the streets in that part of town for years.
I'd had my little run-ins with them in the past. Something told me tonight was going to be different.
I don't owe you anything.

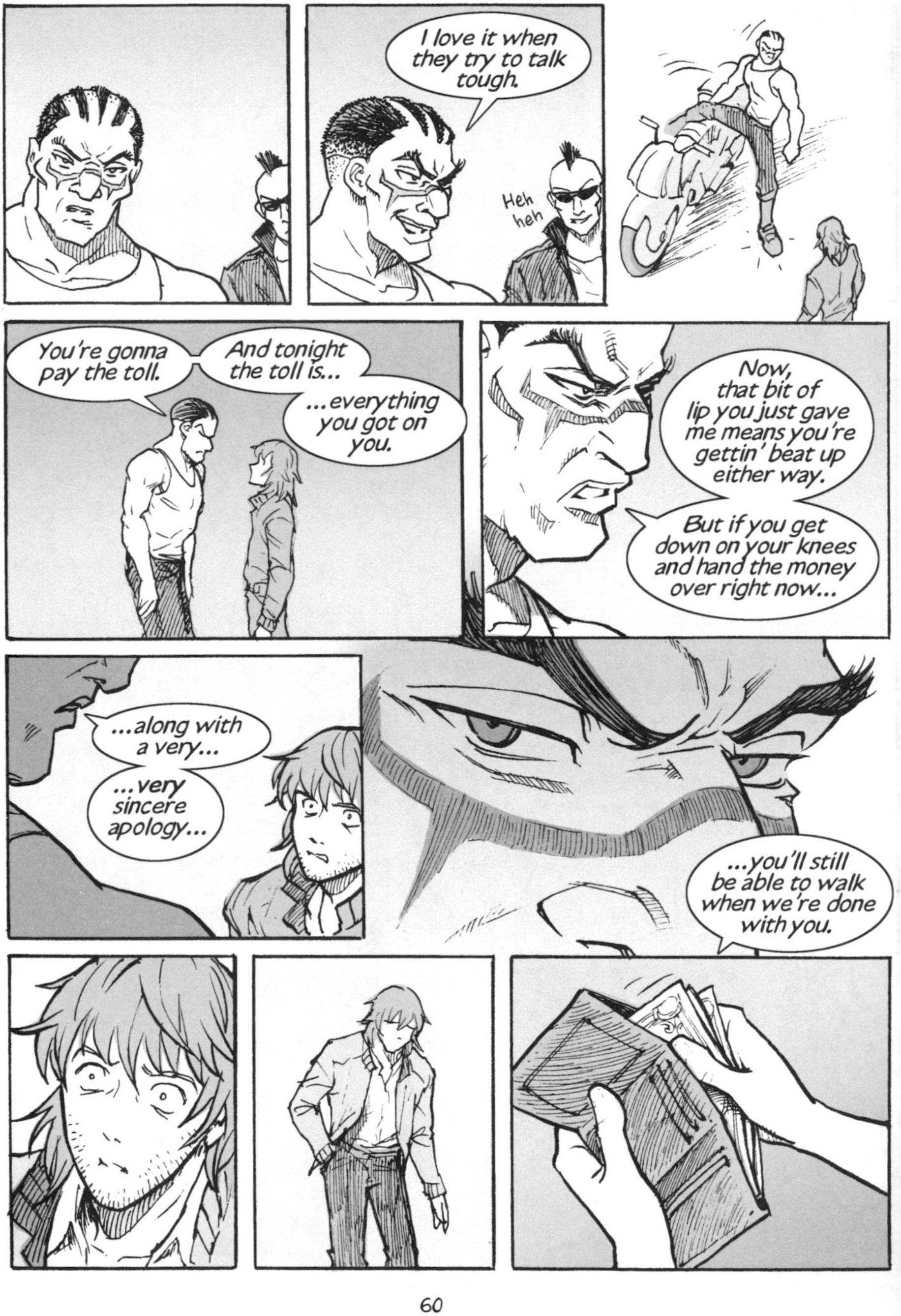
I love it when they try to talk tough.
Heh heh
You're gonna pay the toll.
And tonight the toll is...
...everything you got on you.
Now, that bit of lip you just gave me means you're gettin' beat up either way.
But if you get down on your knees and hand the money over right now...
...along with a very...
...very sincere apology...
...you'll still be able to walk when we're done with you.

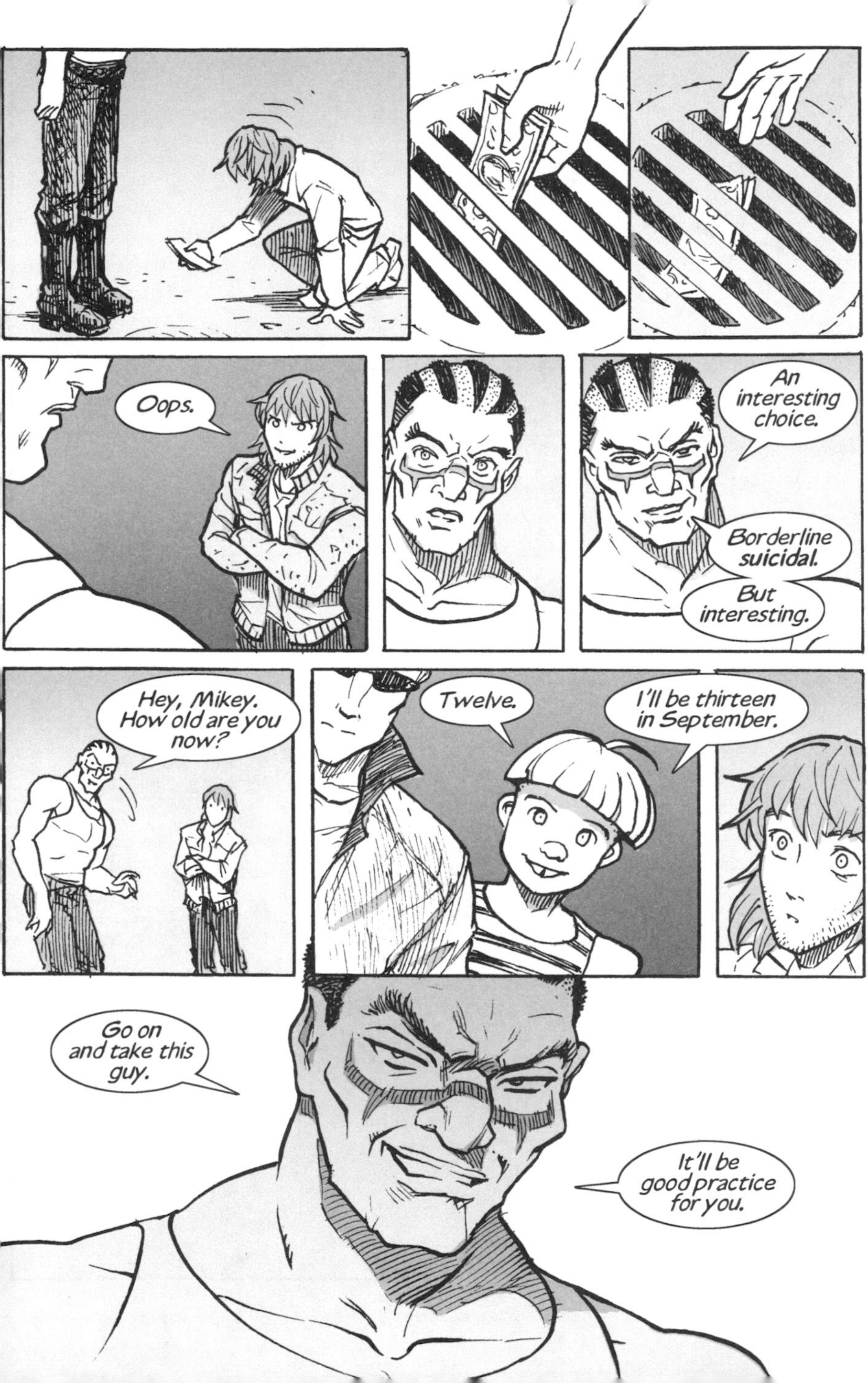
Oops.
An interesting choice.
Borderline **suicidal.**
But interesting.
Hey, Mikey. How old are you now?
Twelve.
I'll be thirteen in September.
Go on and take this guy.
It'll be good practice for you.

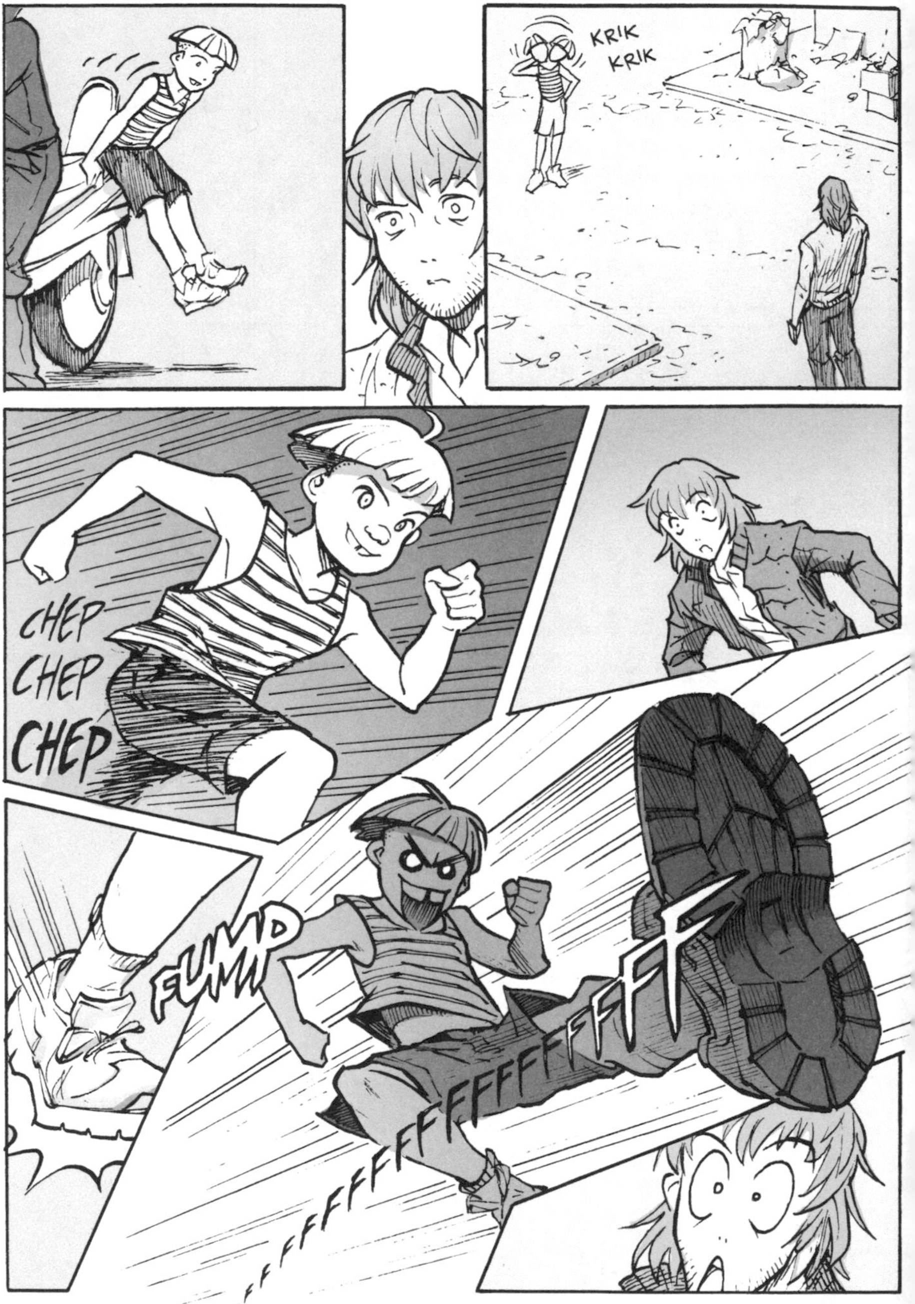
KRIK
KRIK
CHEP
CHEP
CHEP
FUMP
FFFFFFFFFFFFFFFFFFF

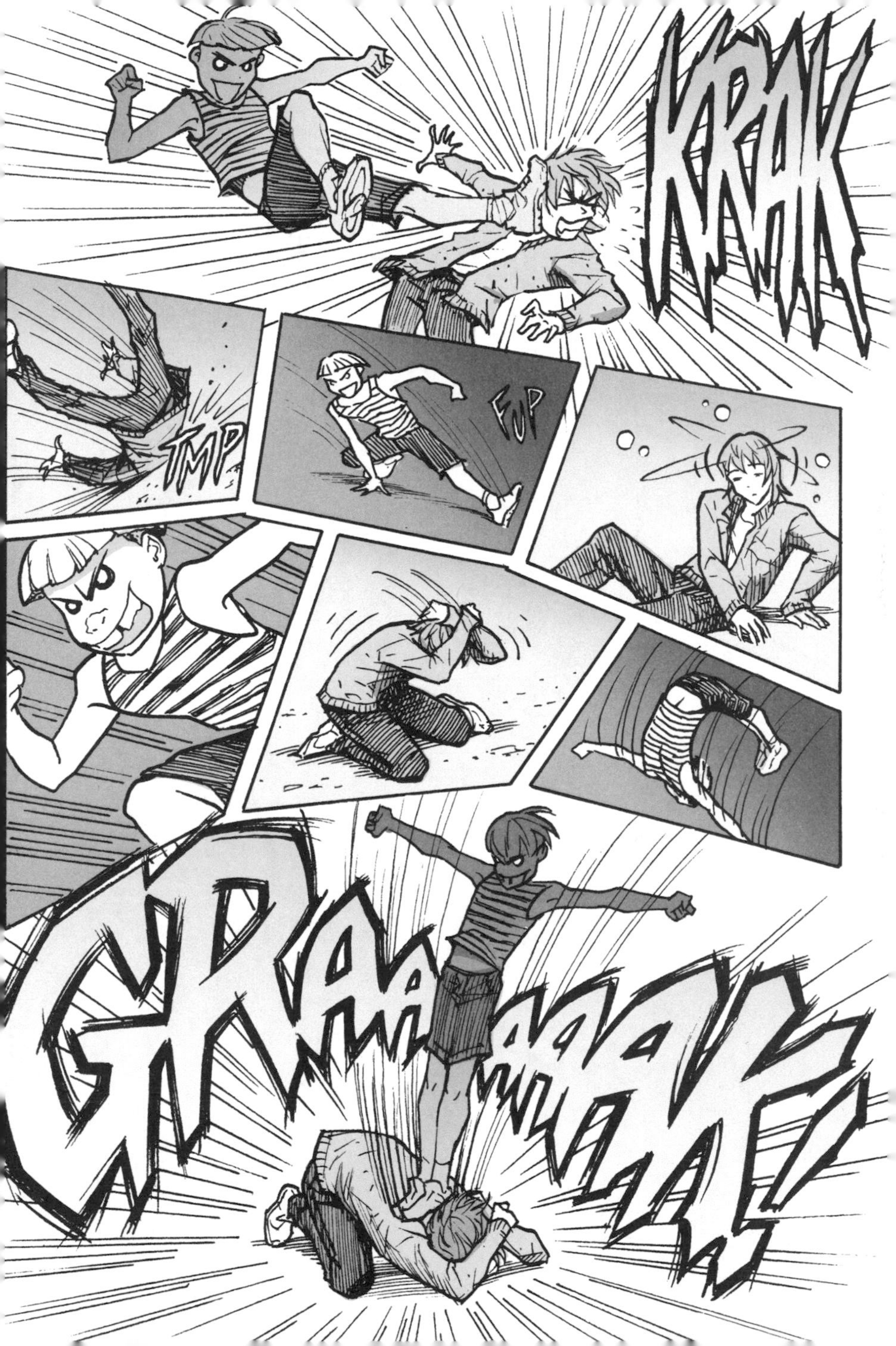
KRAK
TMP
FUP
GRAAAAAK!!

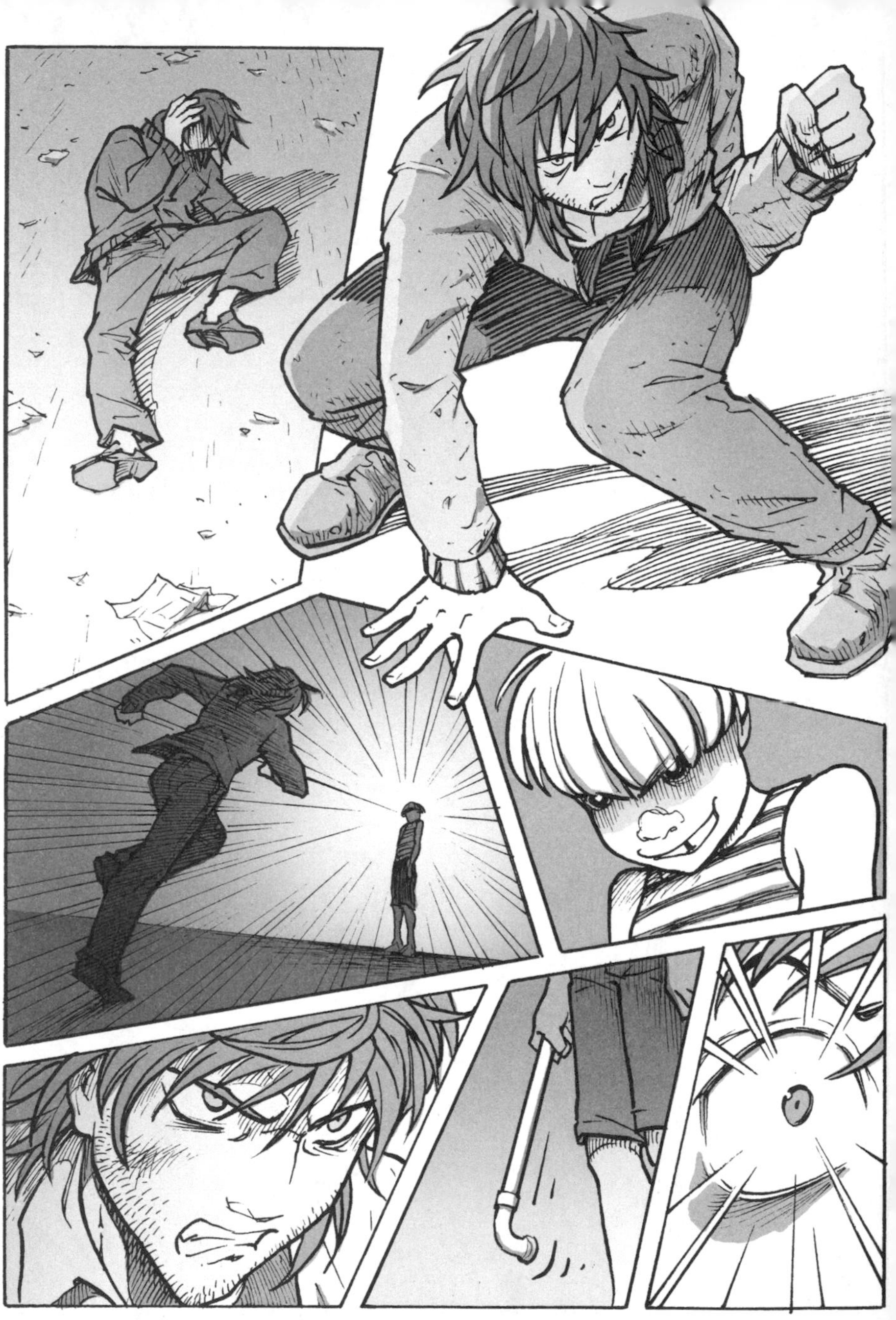

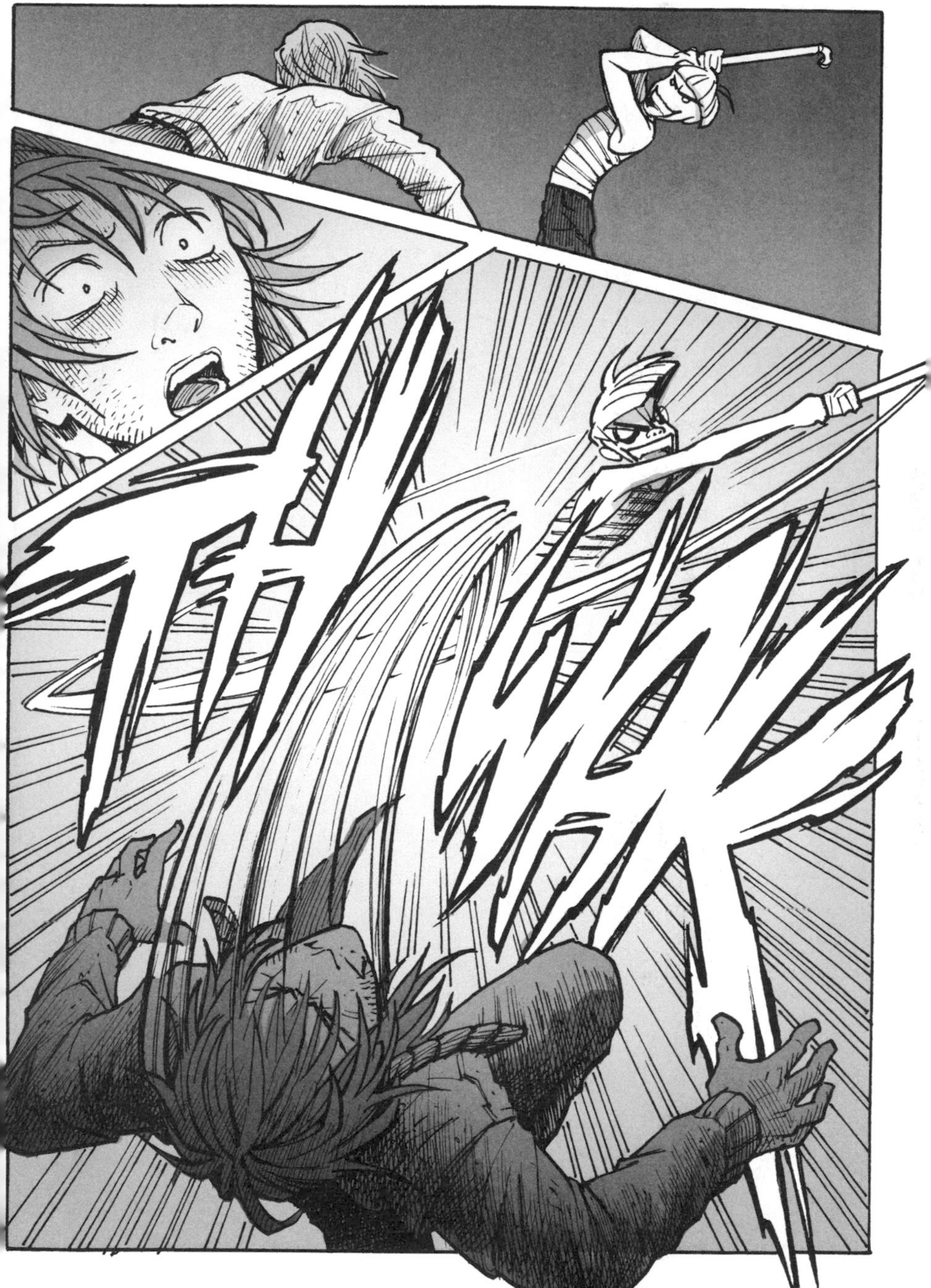
THWAK

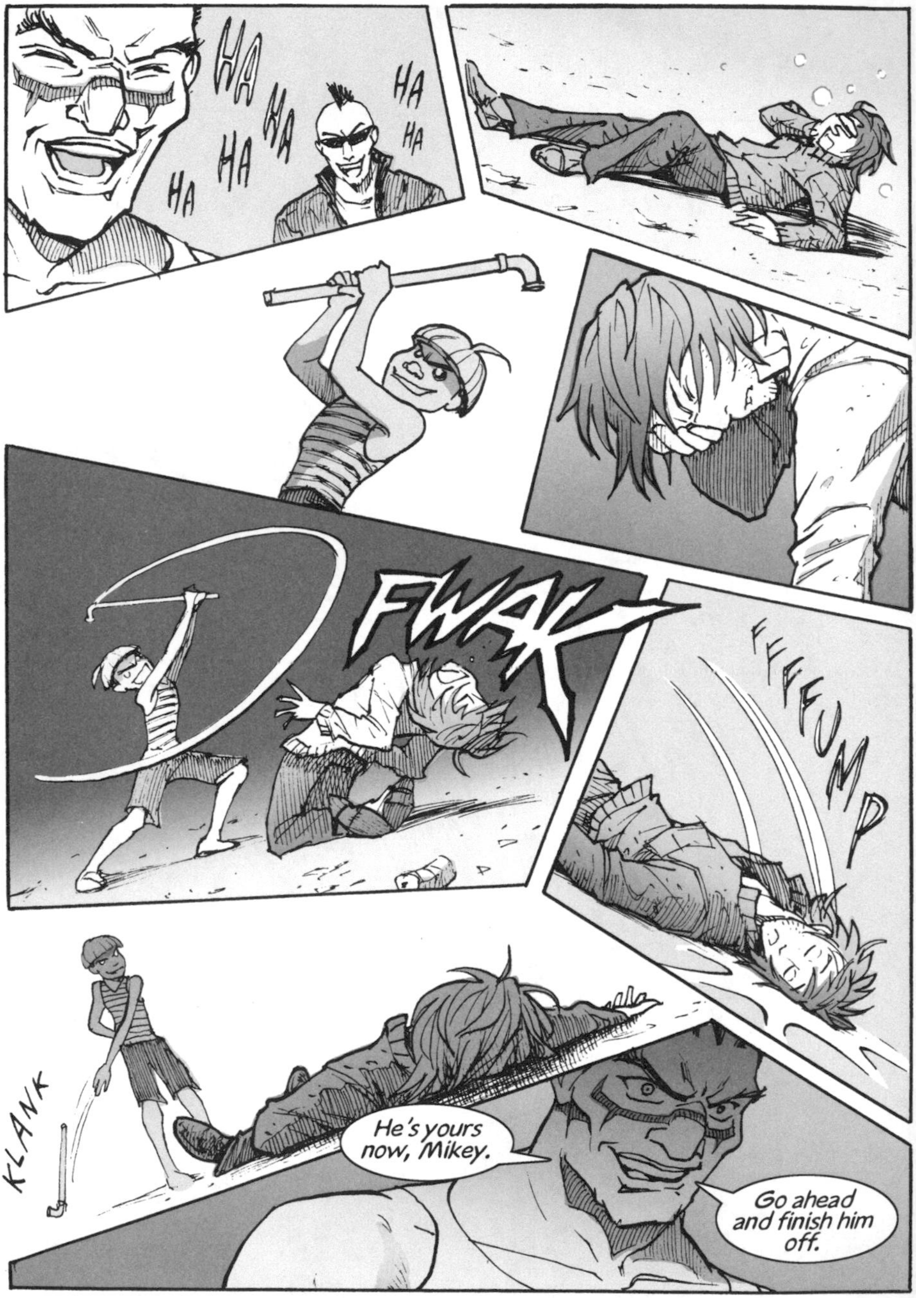
HA HA HA HA HA
HA HA HA
FWAK
FFFFUMP
KLANK
He's yours now, Mikey.
Go ahead and finish him off.

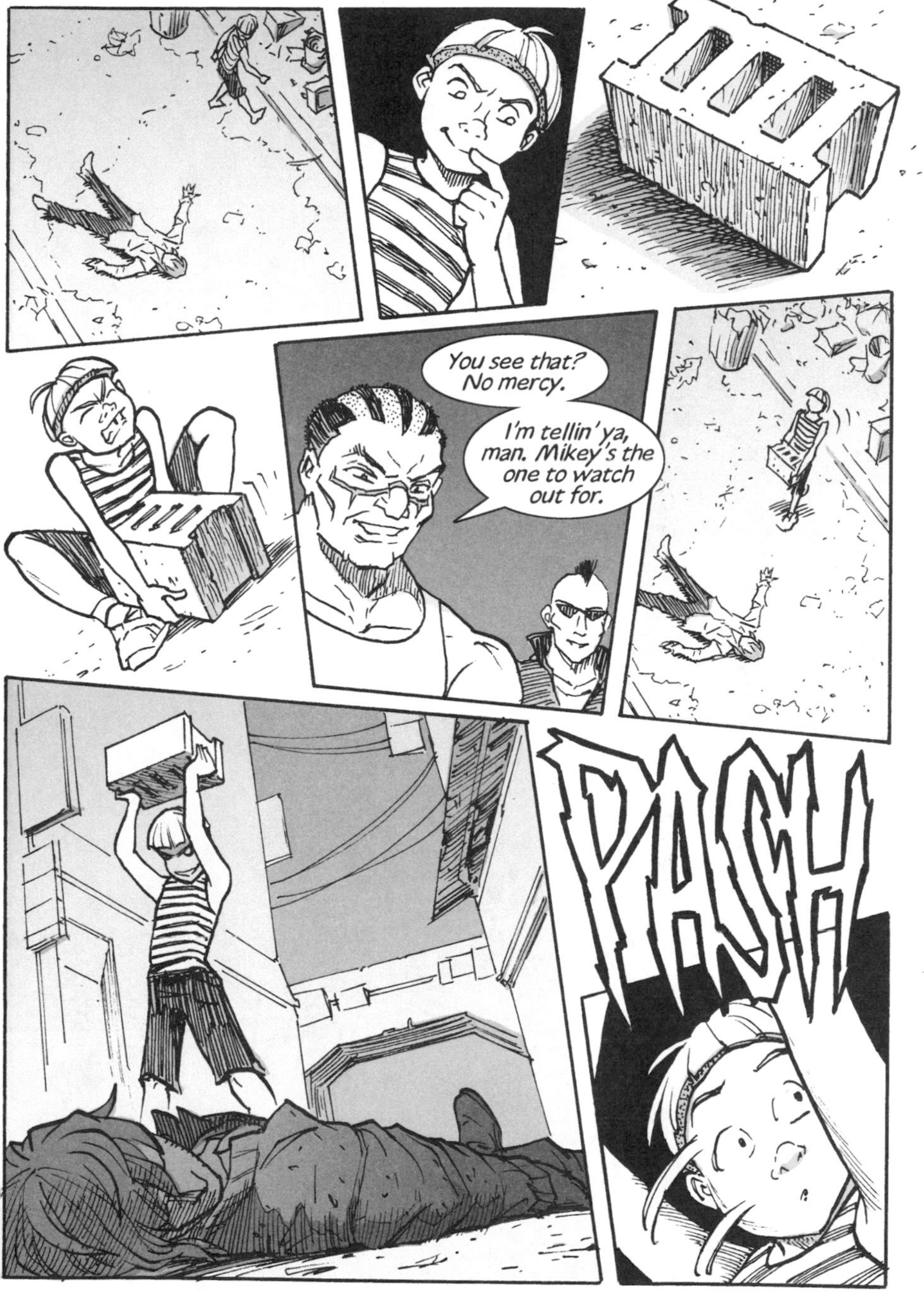
You see that? No mercy.
I'm tellin' ya, man. Mikey's the one to watch out for.
PASH

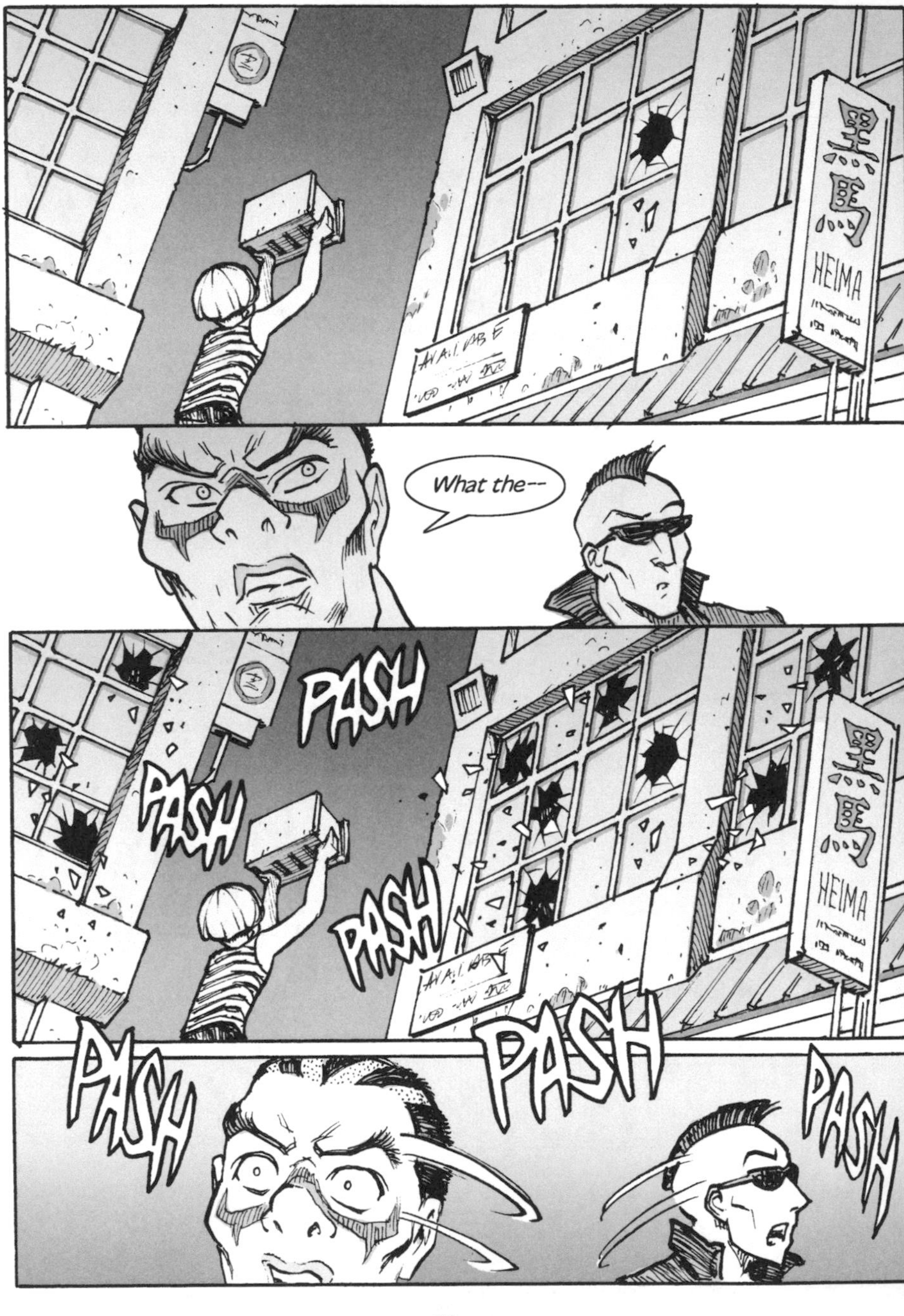
HEIMA
What the--
PASH
PASH
PASH
HEIMA
PASH
PASH
PASH

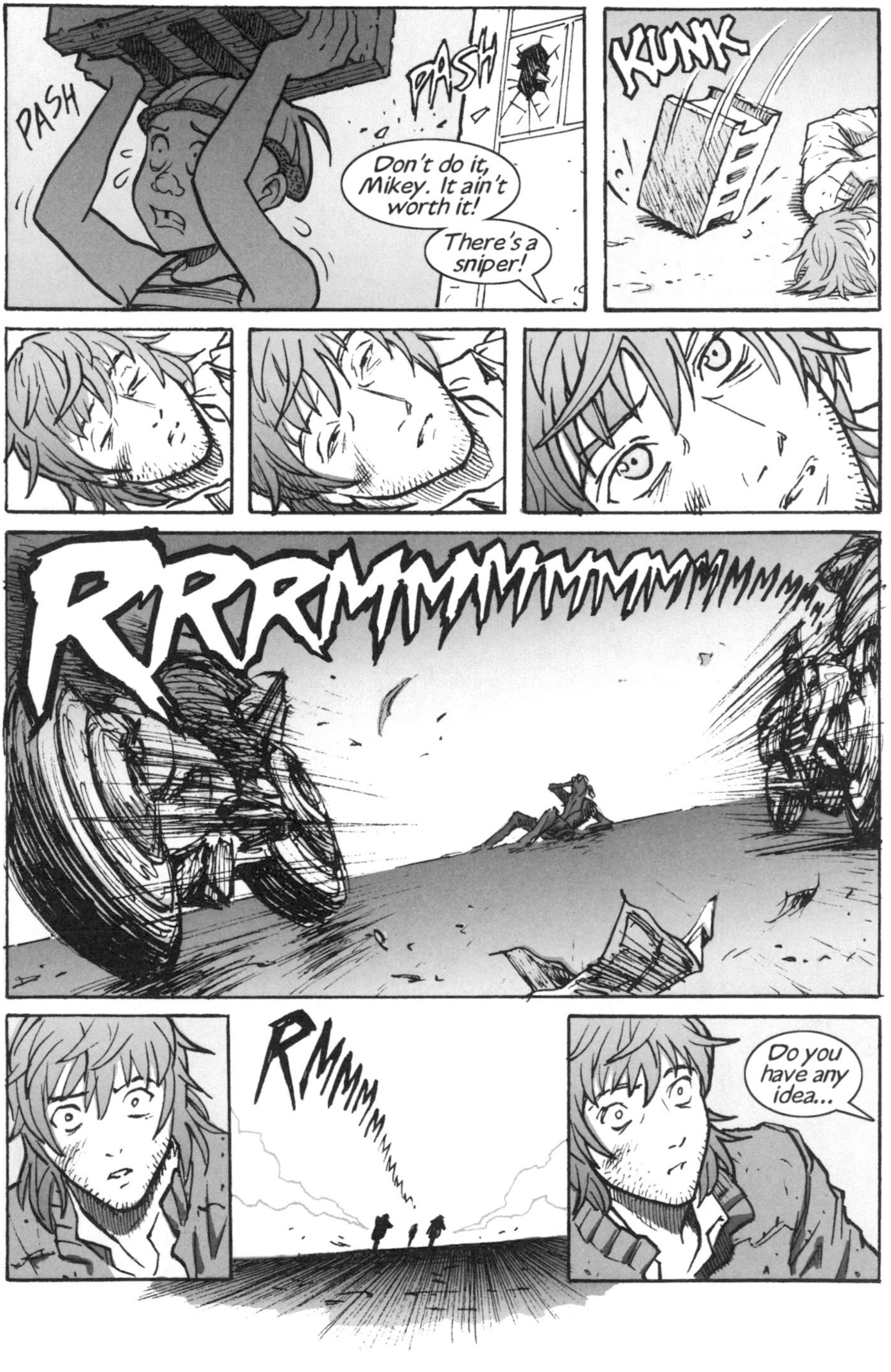
PASH
PASH
Don't do it, Mikey. It ain't worth it!
There's a sniper!
KUNK
RRRMMMMMMMMMMMMMM
RMMMM
Do you have any idea...

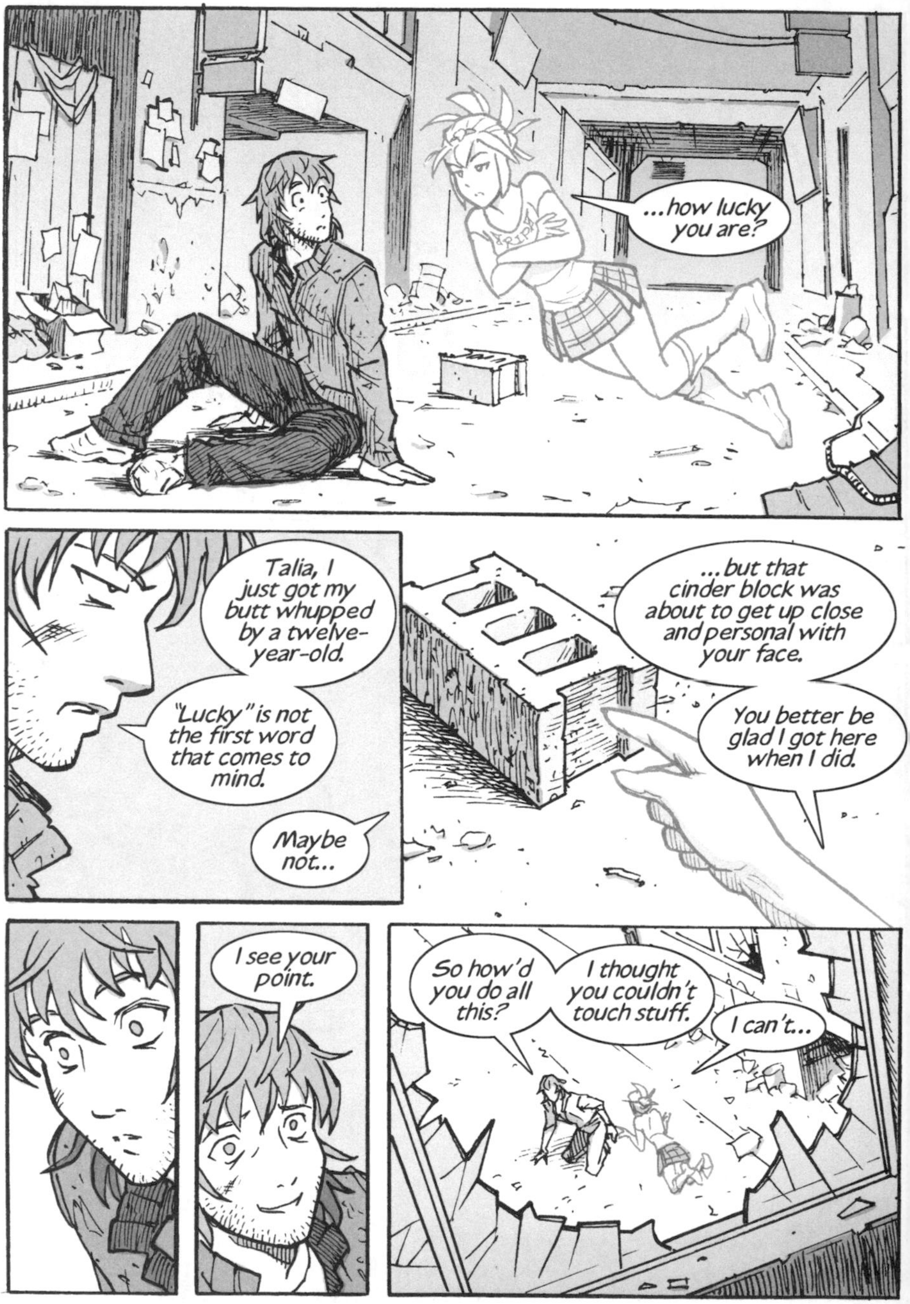
...how lucky you are?
Talia, I just got my butt whupped by a twelve-year-old.
"Lucky" is not the first word that comes to mind.
...but that cinder block was about to get up close and personal with your face.
You better be glad I got here when I did.
Maybe not...
I see your point.
So how'd you do all this?
I thought you couldn't touch stuff.
I can't...

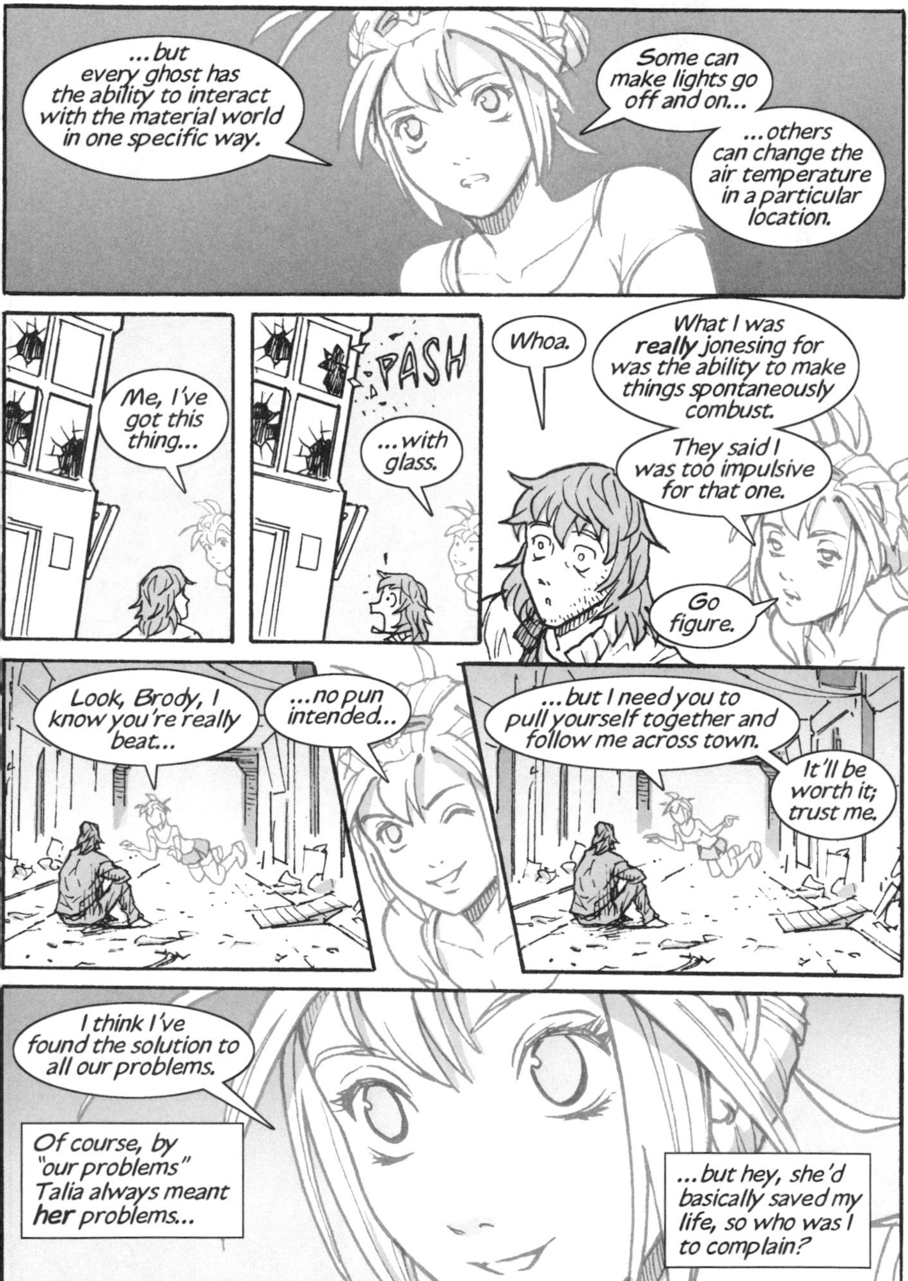
...but every ghost has the ability to interact with the material world in one specific way.
Some can make lights go off and on...
...others can change the air temperature in a particular location.
Me, I've got this thing...
PASH
...with glass.
Whoa.
What I was **really** jonesing for was the ability to make things spontaneously combust.
They said I was too impulsive for that one.
Go figure.
Look, Brody, I know you're really beat...
...no pun intended...
...but I need you to pull yourself together and follow me across town.
It'll be worth it; trust me.
I think I've found the solution to all our problems.
Of course, by "our problems" Talia always meant **her** problems...
...but hey, she'd basically saved my life, so who was I to complain?

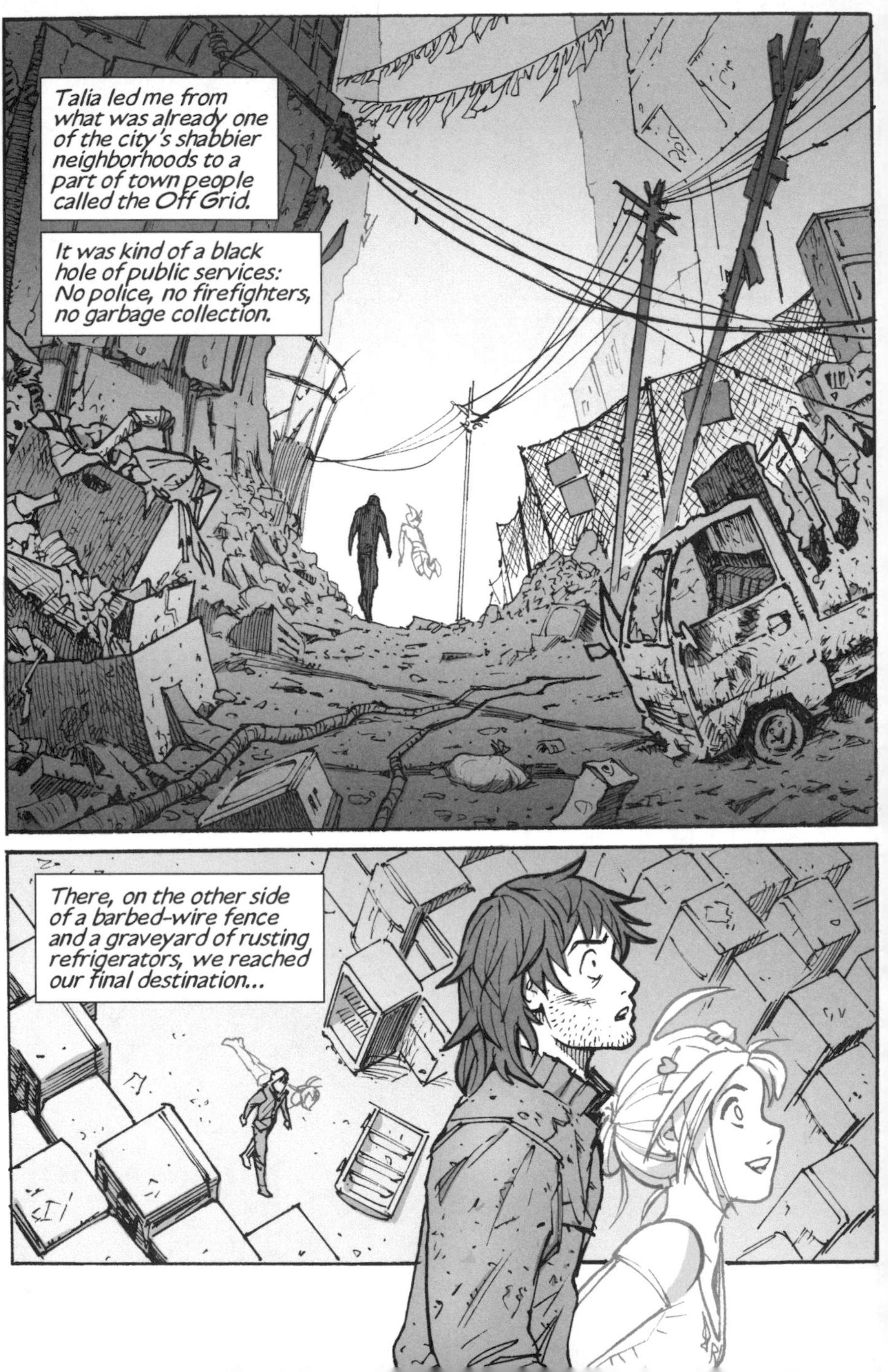
Talia led me from what was already one of the city's shabbier neighborhoods to a part of town people called the Off Grid.
It was kind of a black hole of public services: No police, no firefighters, no garbage collection.
There, on the other side of a barbed-wire fence and a graveyard of rusting refrigerators, we reached our final destination...

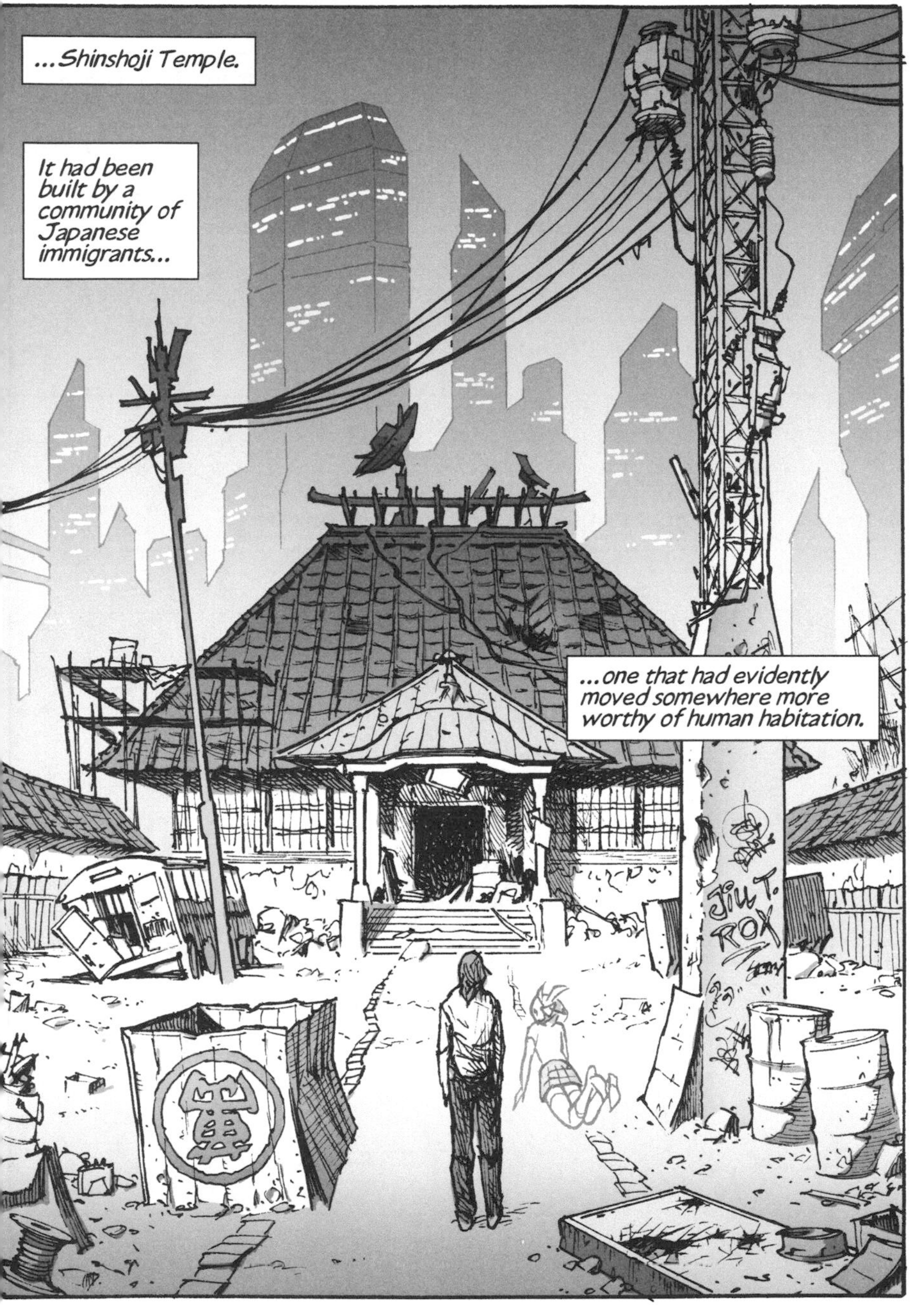
...Shinshoji Temple.
It had been built by a community of Japanese immigrants...
...one that had evidently moved somewhere more worthy of human habitation.
JILL T. ROX

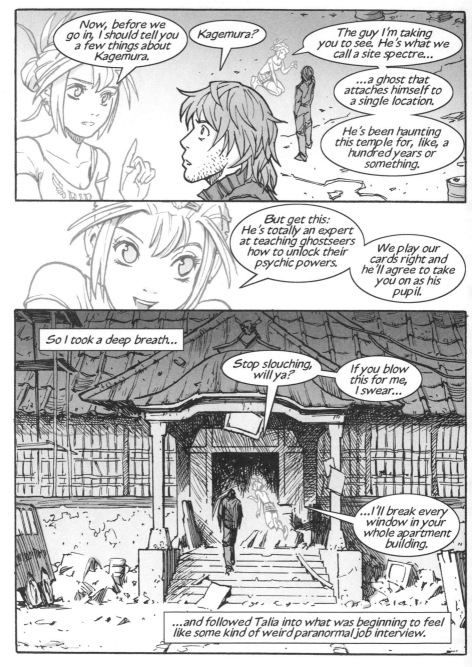

Now, before we go in, I should tell you a few things about Kagemura.

Kagemura?

The guy I'm taking you to see. He's what we call a site spectre...

...a ghost that attaches himself to a single location.

He's been haunting this temple for, like, a hundred years or something.

But get this: He's totally an expert at teaching ghostseers how to unlock their psychic powers.

We play our cards right and he'll agree to take you on as his pupil.

So I took a deep breath...

Stop slouching, will ya?

If you blow this for me, I swear...

...I'll break every window in your whole apartment building.

...and followed Talia into what was beginning to feel like some kind of weird paranormal job interview.

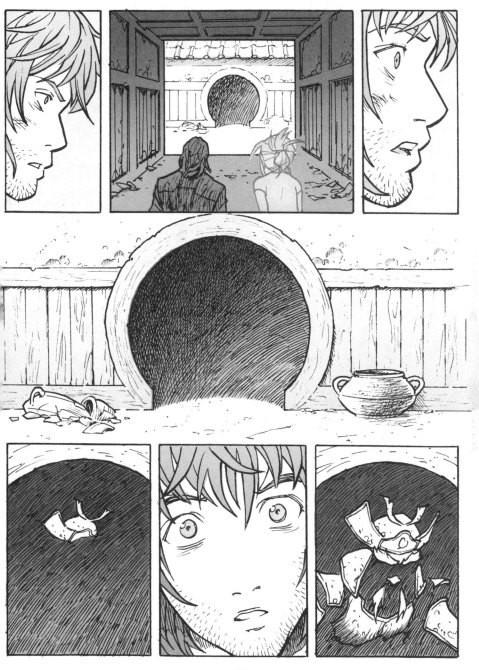

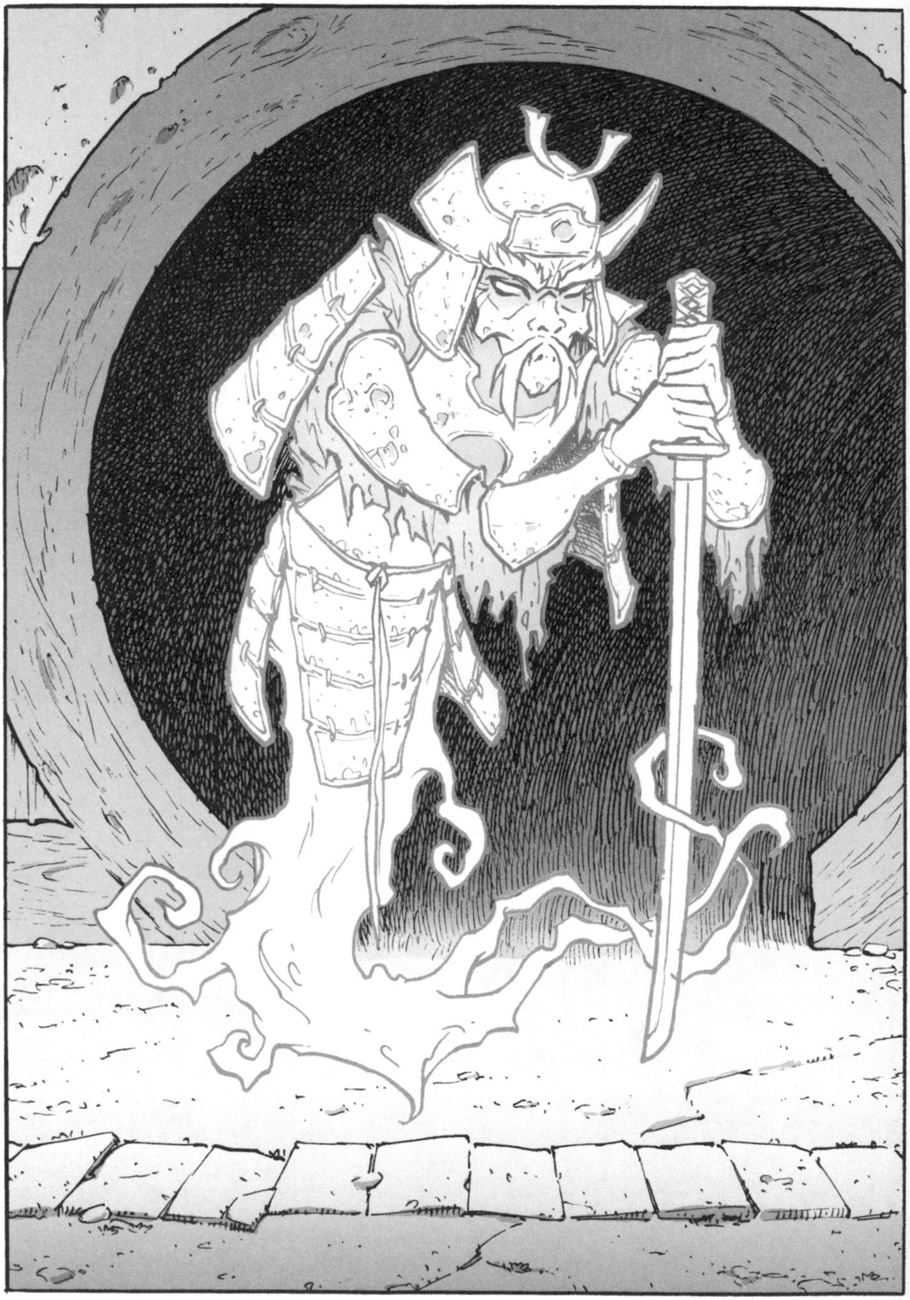

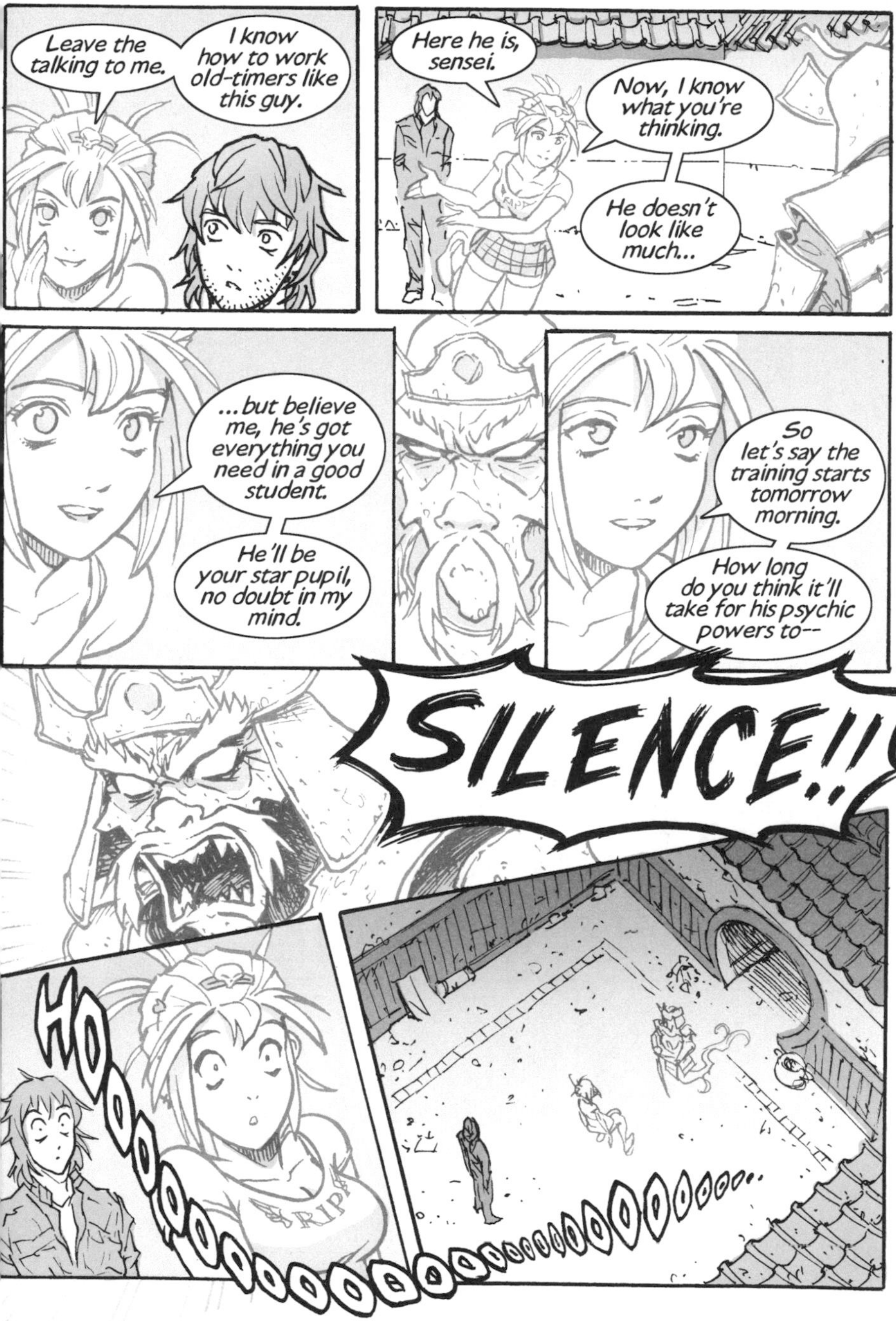
Leave the talking to me.
I know how to work old-timers like this guy.
Here he is, sensei.
Now, I know what you're thinking.
He doesn't look like much...
...but believe me, he's got everything you need in a good student.
He'll be your star pupil, no doubt in my mind.
So let's say the training starts tomorrow morning.
How long do you think it'll take for his psychic powers to--
SILENCE!!
HOOOOOOOOOOOOOOOOOOOOOOOOOOOO...

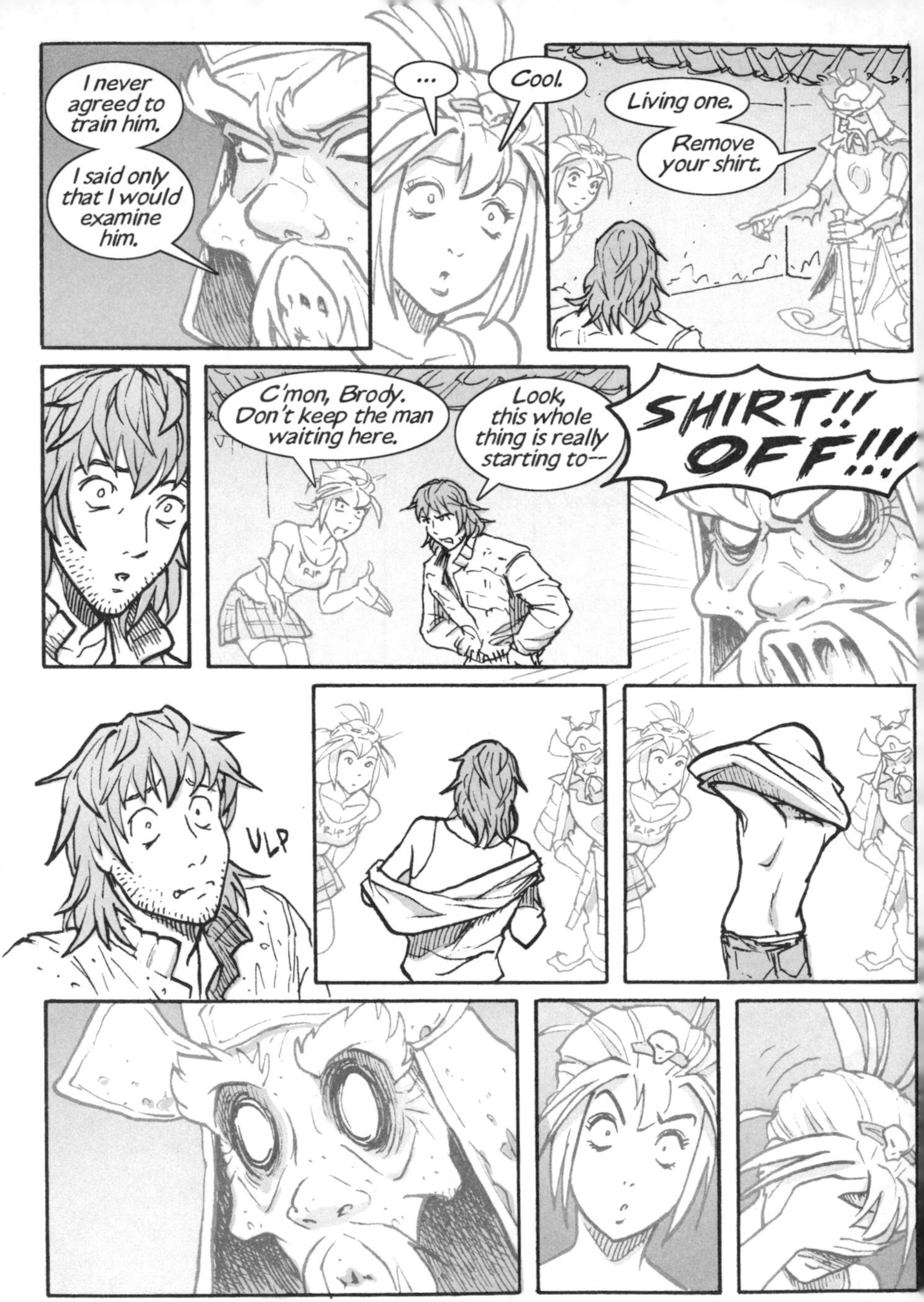
I never agreed to train him.
I said only that I would examine him.
...
Cool.
Living one.
Remove your shirt.
C'mon, Brody. Don't keep the man waiting here.
Look, this whole thing is really starting to--
SHIRT!! OFF!!!
ULP

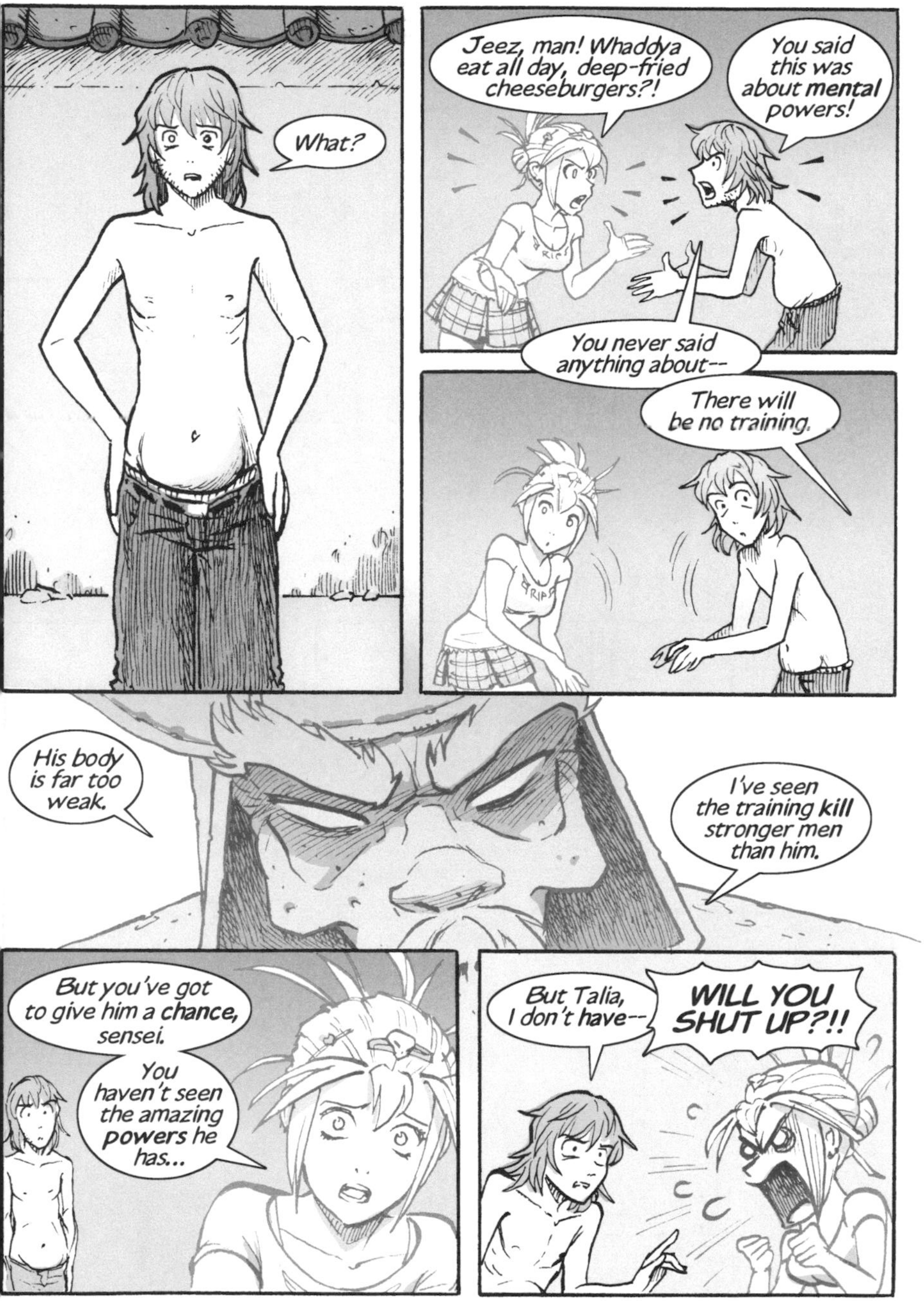
What?
Jeez, man! Whaddya eat all day, deep-fried cheeseburgers?!
You said this was about mental powers!
You never said anything about--
There will be no training.
His body is far too weak.
I've seen the training kill stronger men than him.
But you've got to give him a chance, sensei.
You haven't seen the amazing powers he has...
But Talia, I don't have--
WILL YOU SHUT UP?!!

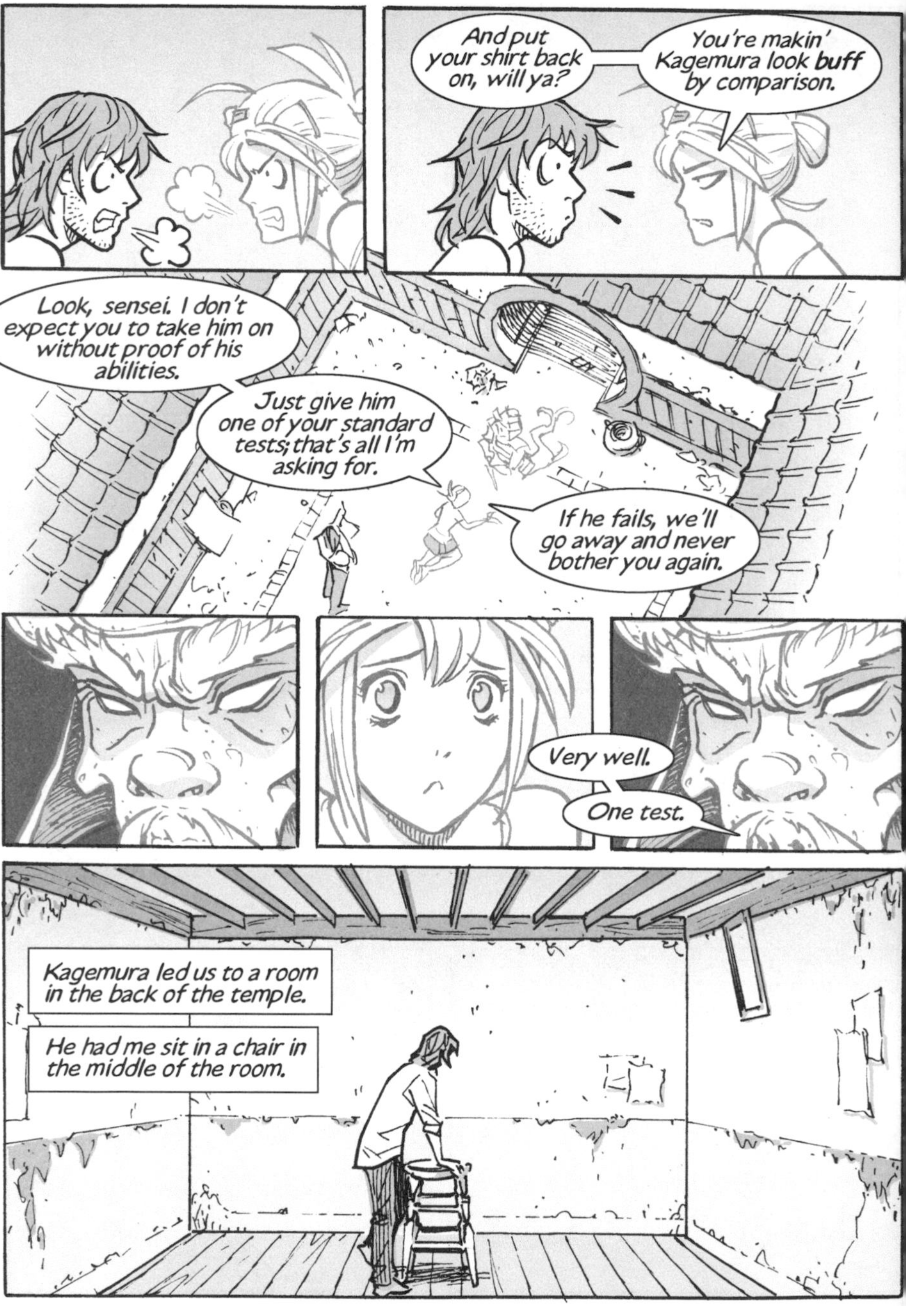
And put your shirt back on, will ya?
You're makin' Kagemura look **buff** by comparison.
Look, sensei. I don't expect you to take him on without proof of his abilities.
Just give him one of your standard tests; that's all I'm asking for.
If he fails, we'll go away and never bother you again.
Very well.
One test.
Kagemura led us to a room in the back of the temple.
He had me sit in a chair in the middle of the room.

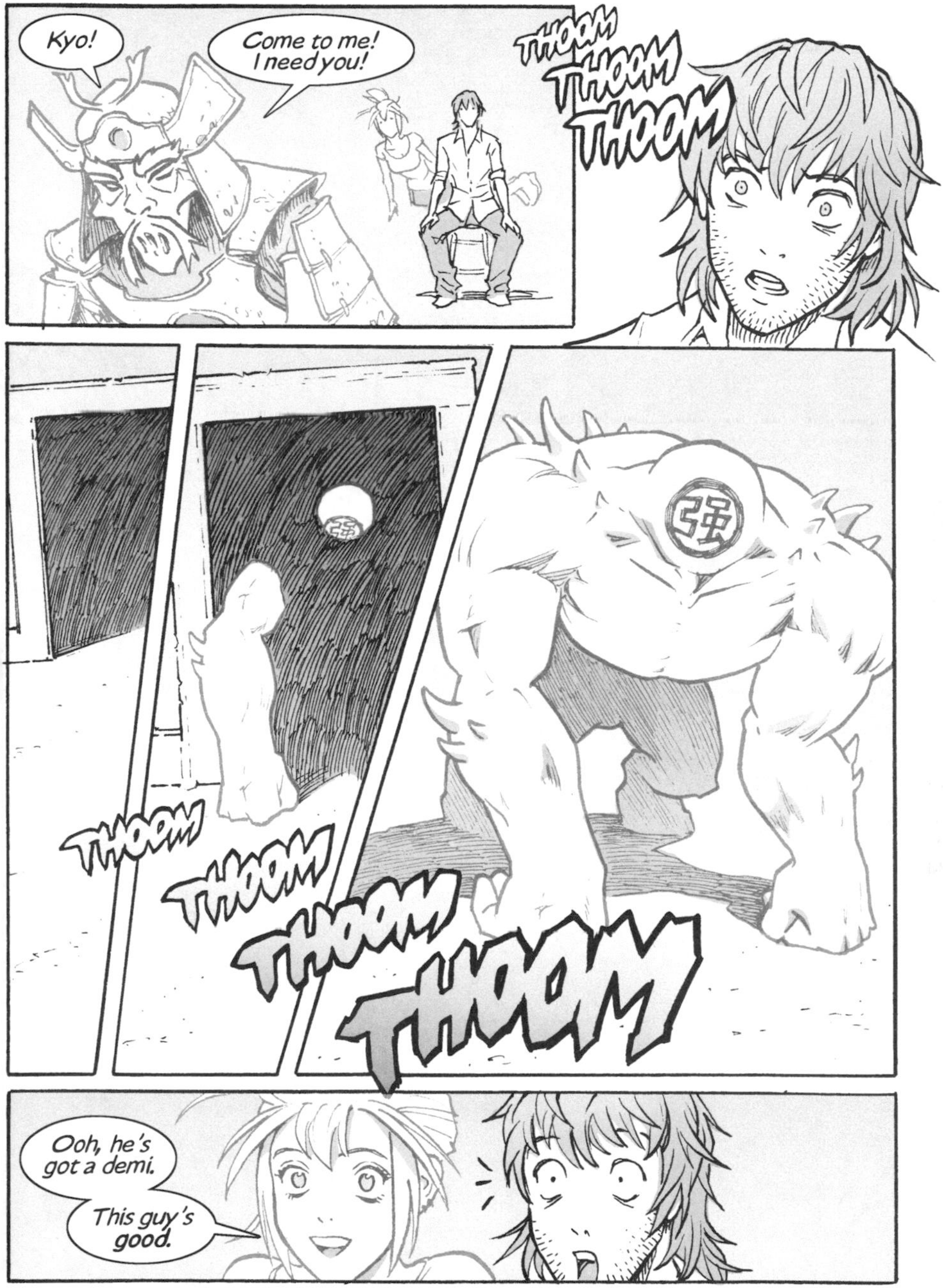
Kyo!
Come to me! I need you!
THOOM
THOOM
THOOM
THOOM
THOOM
THOOM
THOOM
Ooh, he's got a demi.
This guy's good.

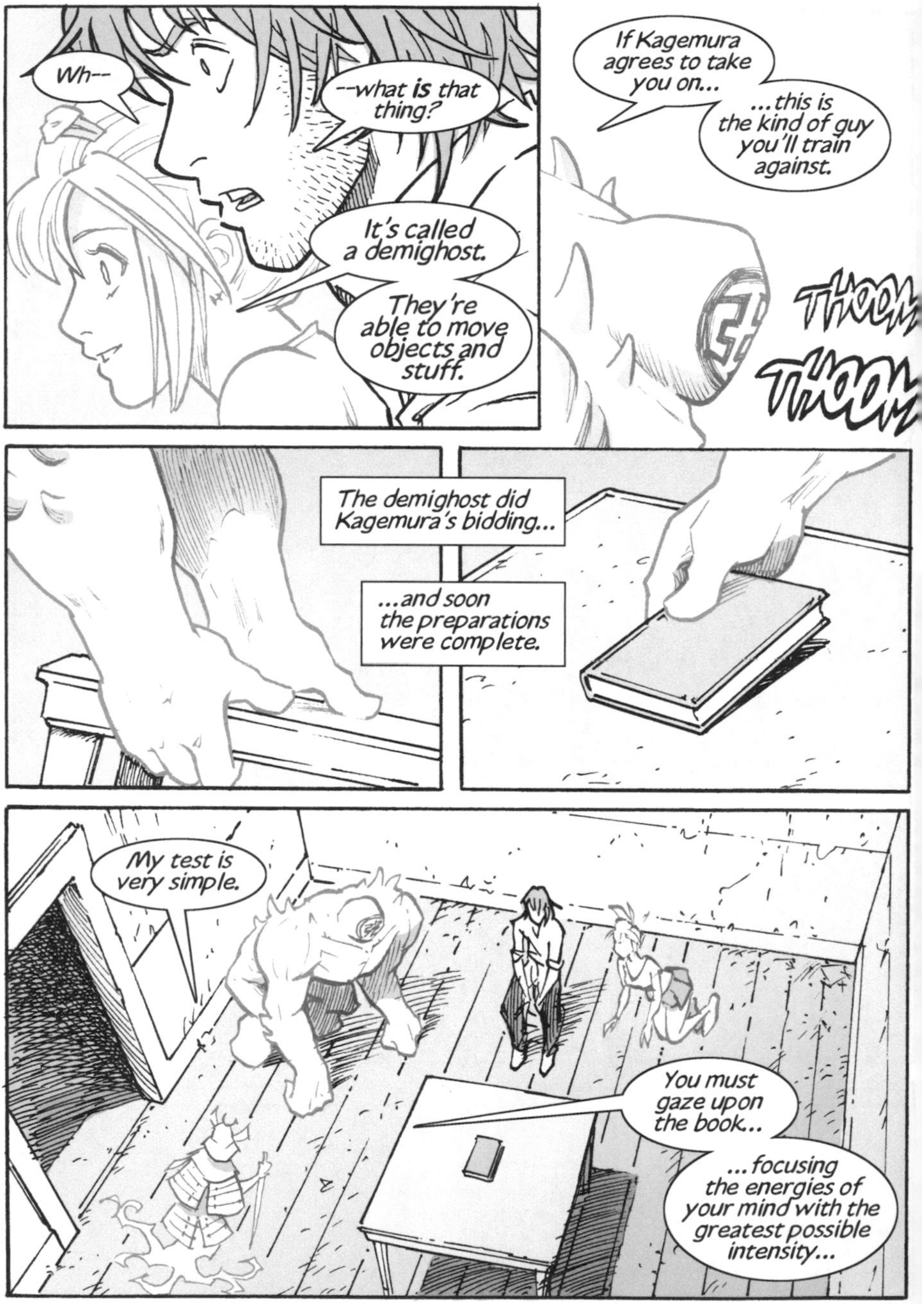
Wh--
--what is that thing?
If Kagemura agrees to take you on...
...this is the kind of guy you'll train against.
It's called a demighost.
They're able to move objects and stuff.
THOOM
THOOM
The demighost did Kagemura's bidding...
...and soon the preparations were complete.
My test is very simple.
You must gaze upon the book...
...focusing the energies of your mind with the greatest possible intensity...

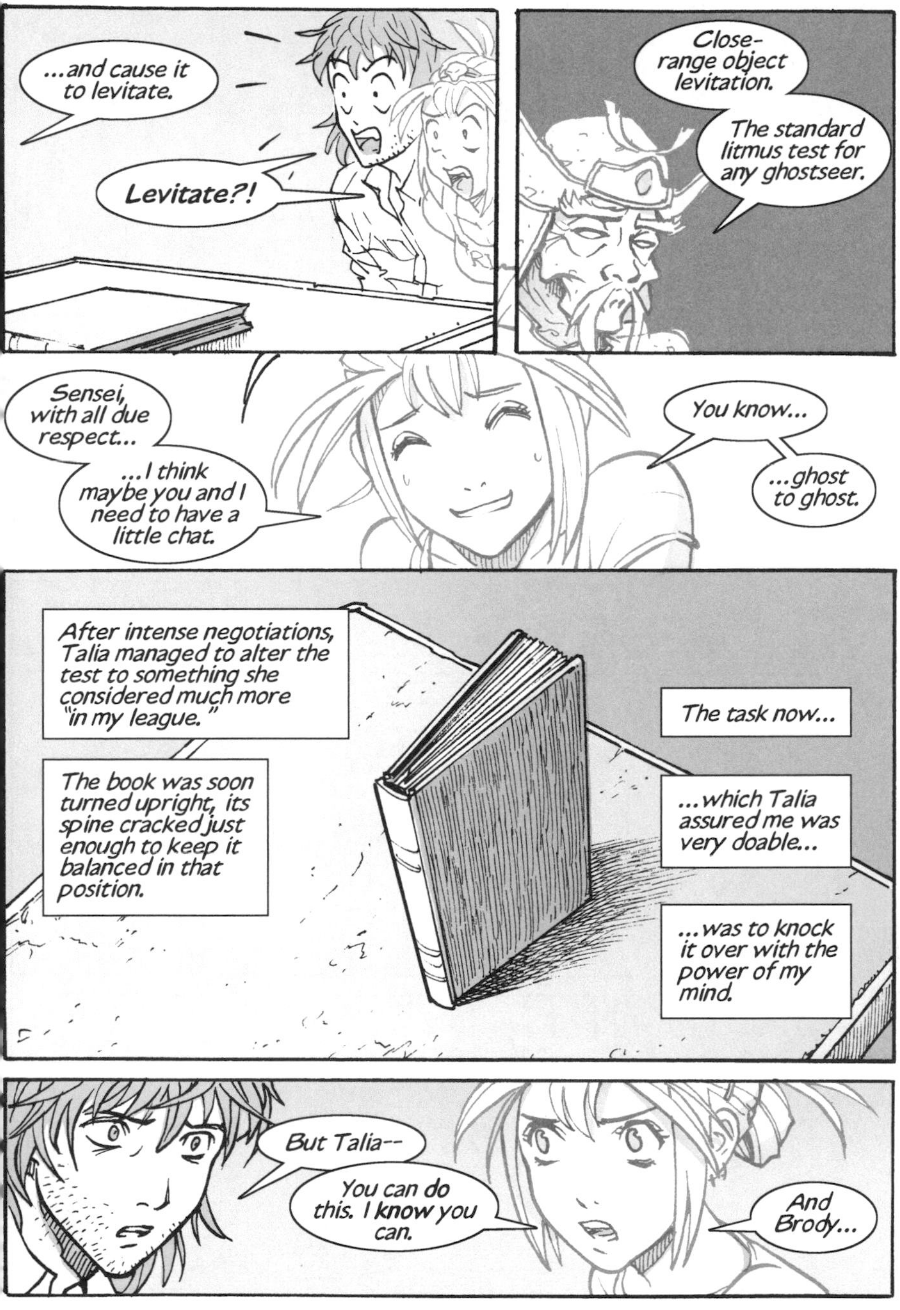
...and cause it to levitate.
Levitate?!
Close-range object levitation.
The standard litmus test for any ghostseer.
Sensei, with all due respect...
...I think maybe you and I need to have a little chat.
You know...
...ghost to ghost.
After intense negotiations, Talia managed to alter the test to something she considered much more "in my league."
The book was soon turned upright, its spine cracked just enough to keep it balanced in that position.
The task now...
...which Talia assured me was very doable...
...was to knock it over with the power of my mind.
But Talia--
You can do this. I know you can.
And Brody...

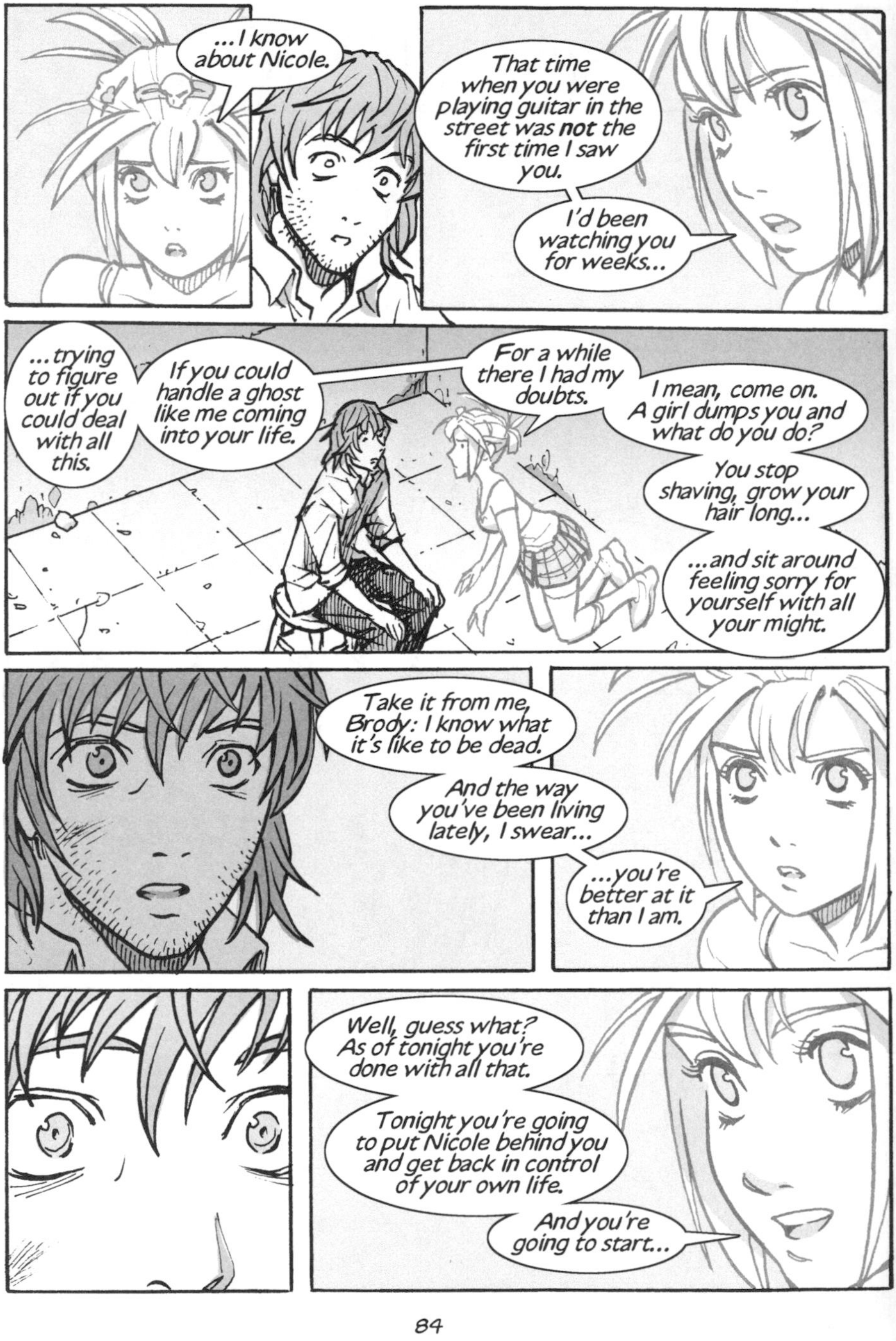
...I know about Nicole.
That time when you were playing guitar in the street was **not** the first time I saw you.
I'd been watching you for weeks...
...trying to figure out if you could deal with all this.
If you could handle a ghost like me coming into your life.
For a while there I had my doubts.
I mean, come on. A girl dumps you and what do you do?
You stop shaving, grow your hair long...
...and sit around feeling sorry for yourself with all your might.
Take it from me, Brody: I know what it's like to be dead.
And the way you've been living lately, I swear...
...you're better at it than I am.
Well, guess what? As of tonight you're done with all that.
Tonight you're going to put Nicole behind you and get back in control of your own life.
And you're going to start...

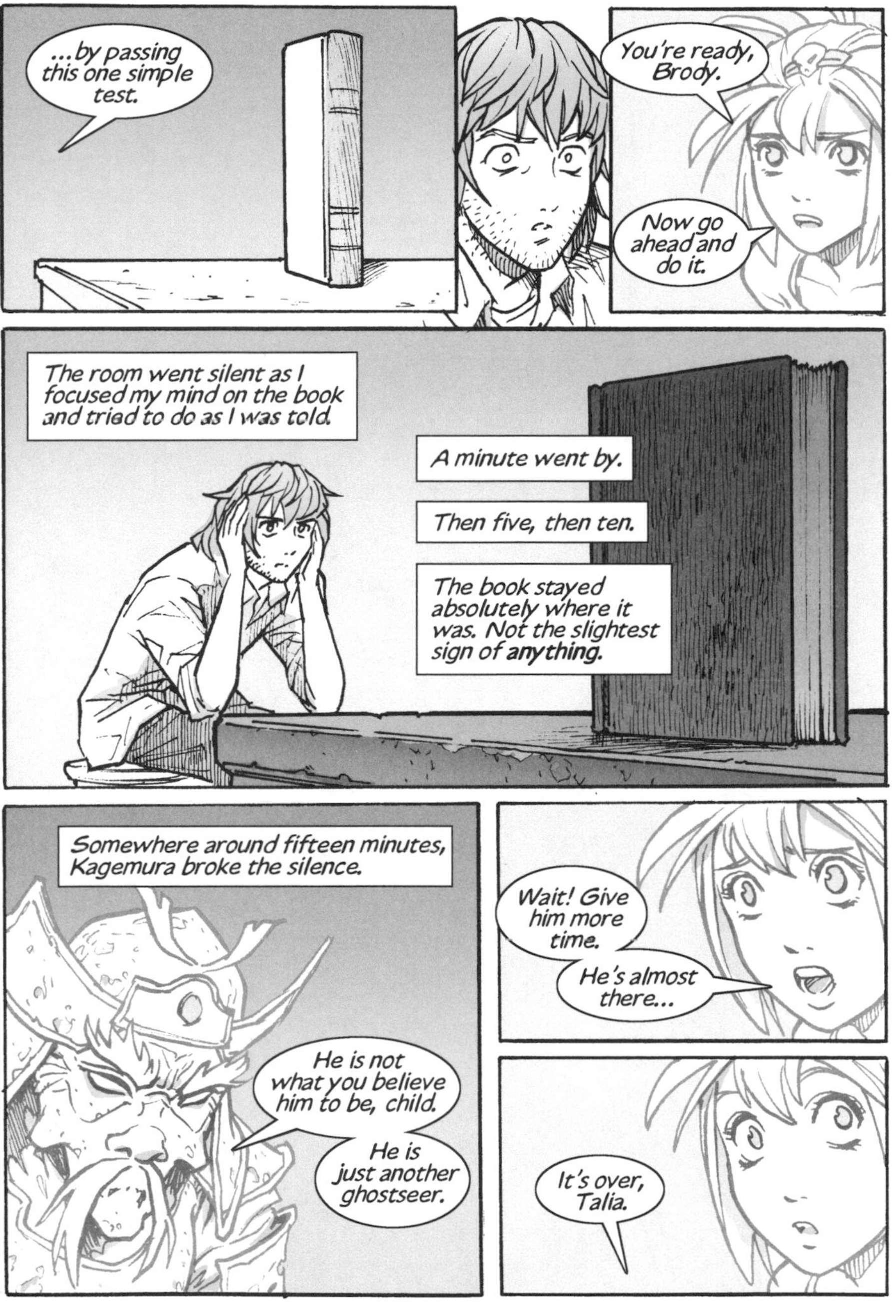
...by passing this one simple test.
You're ready, Brody.
Now go ahead and do it.
The room went silent as I focused my mind on the book and tried to do as I was told.
A minute went by.
Then five, then ten.
The book stayed absolutely where it was. Not the slightest sign of anything.
Somewhere around fifteen minutes, Kagemura broke the silence.
Wait! Give him more time.
He's almost there...
He is not what you believe him to be, child.
He is just another ghostseer.
It's over, Talia.

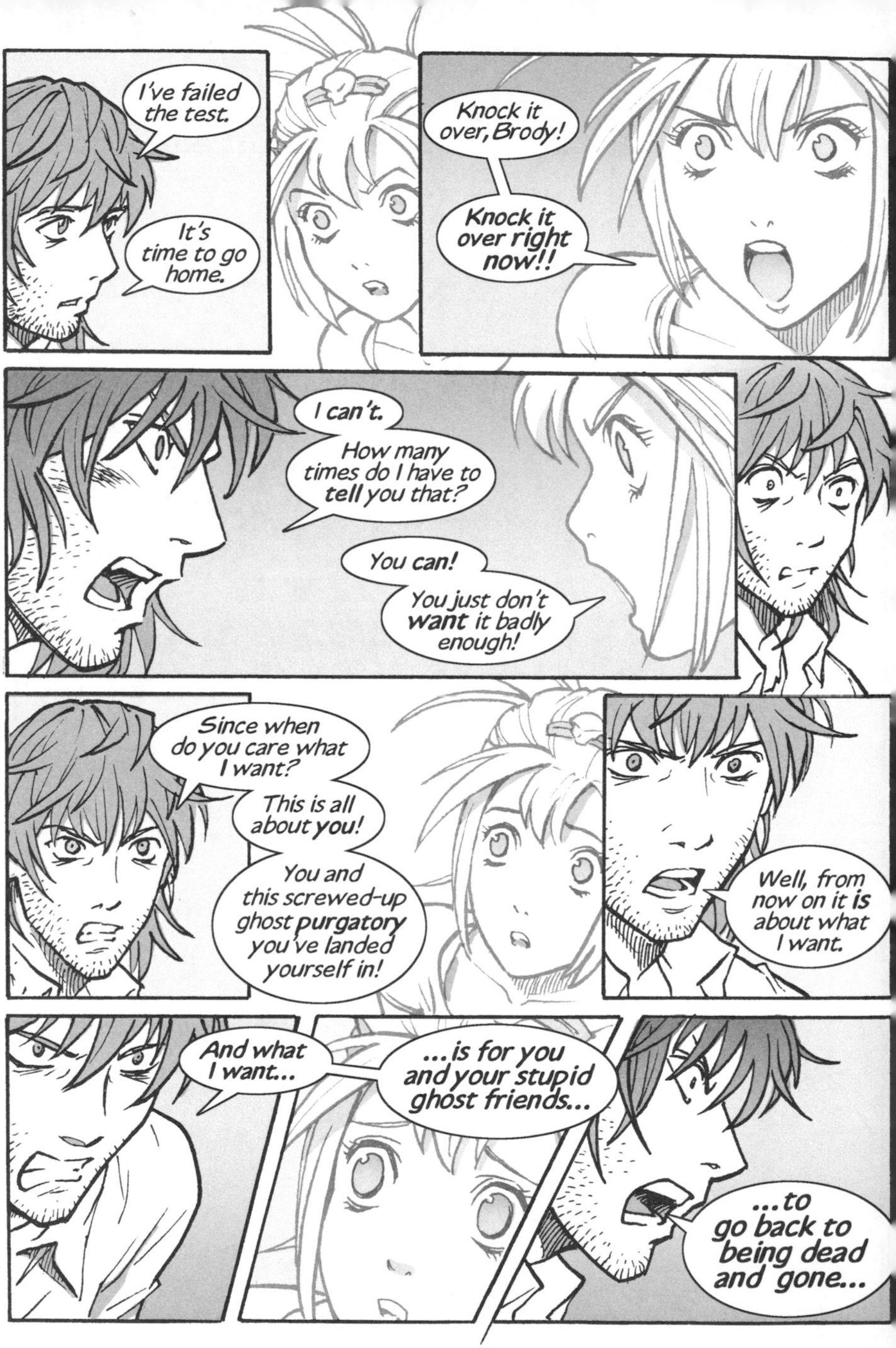
I've failed the test.
It's time to go home.
Knock it over, Brody!
Knock it over right now!!
I can't.
How many times do I have to tell you that?
You can!
You just don't want it badly enough!
Since when do you care what I want?
This is all about you!
You and this screwed-up ghost purgatory you've landed yourself in!
Well, from now on it is about what I want.
And what I want...
...is for you and your stupid ghost friends...
...to go back to being dead and gone...

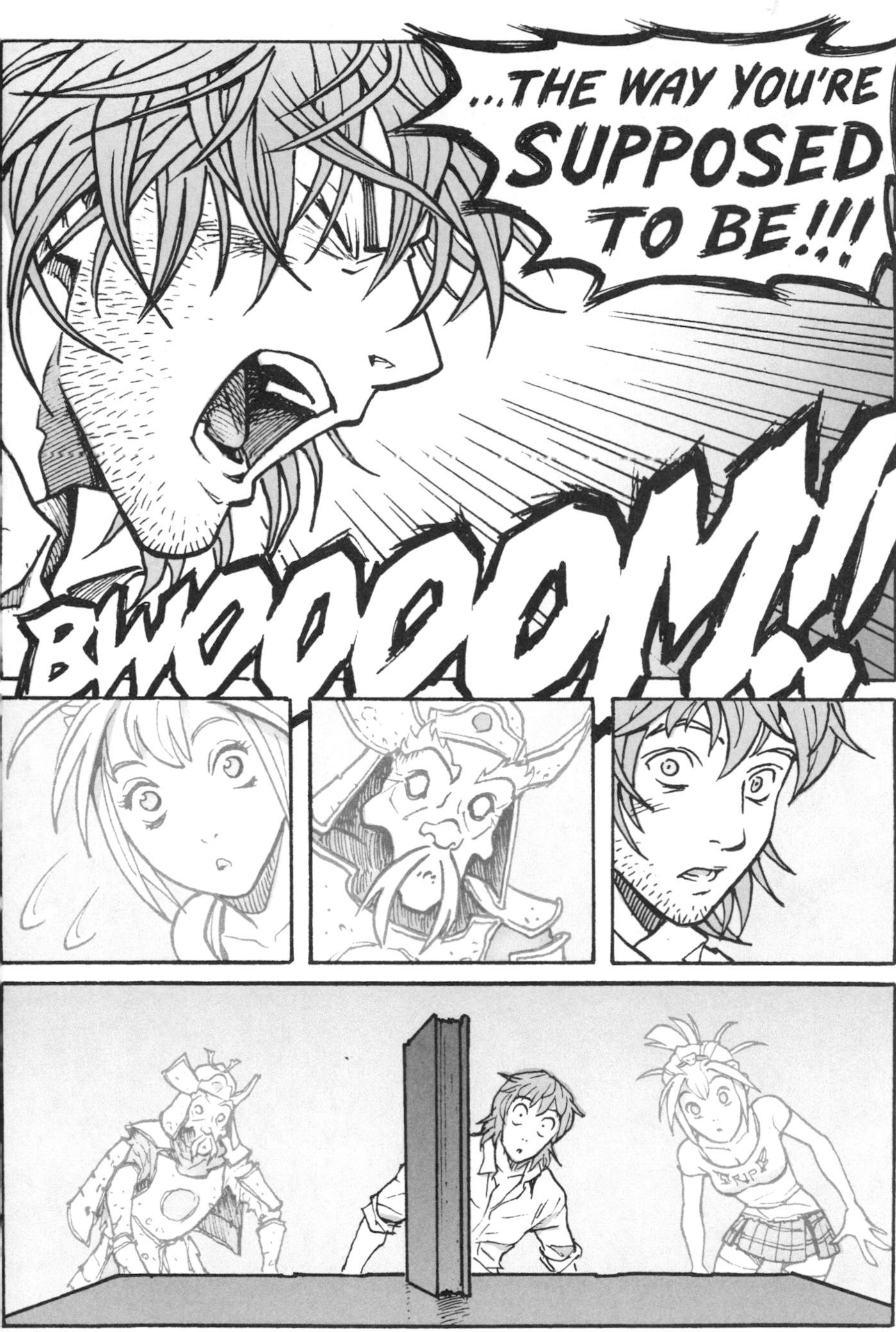
...THE WAY YOU'RE SUPPOSED TO BE!!!
BWOOOOM!!

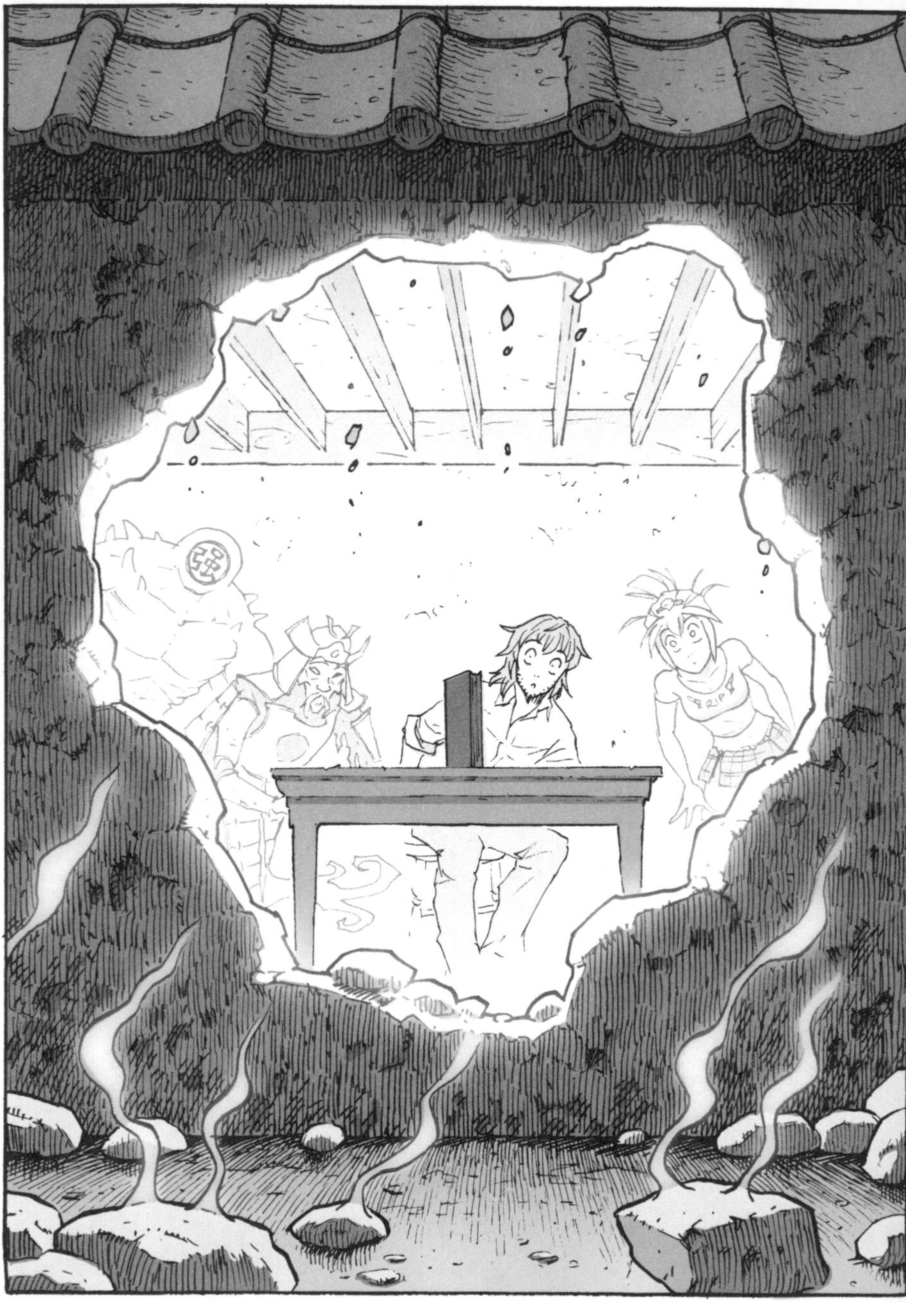

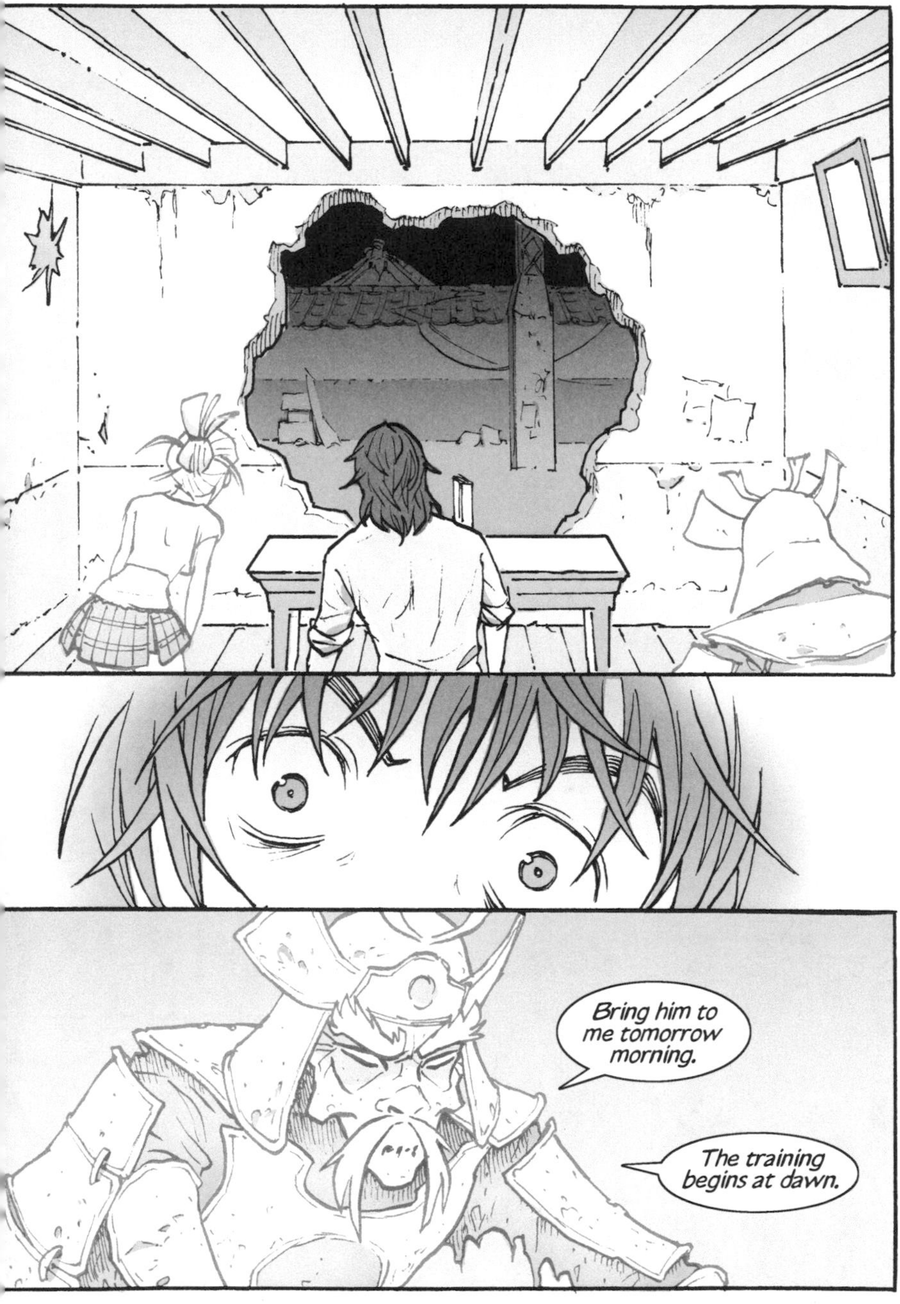
Bring him to me tomorrow morning.
The training begins at dawn.

TO BE CONTINUED IN BRODY'S GHOST BOOK TWO...

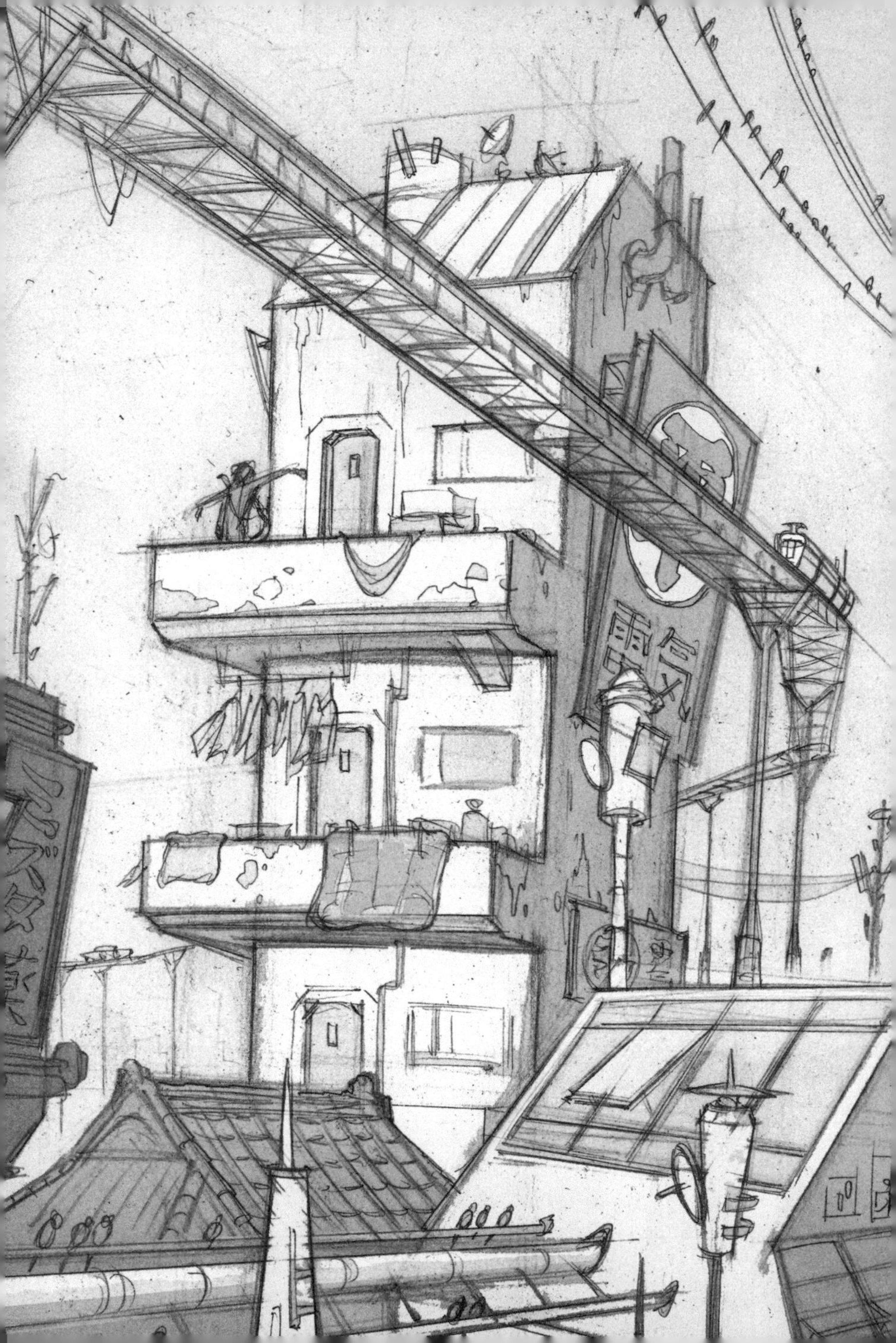

SKETCHES

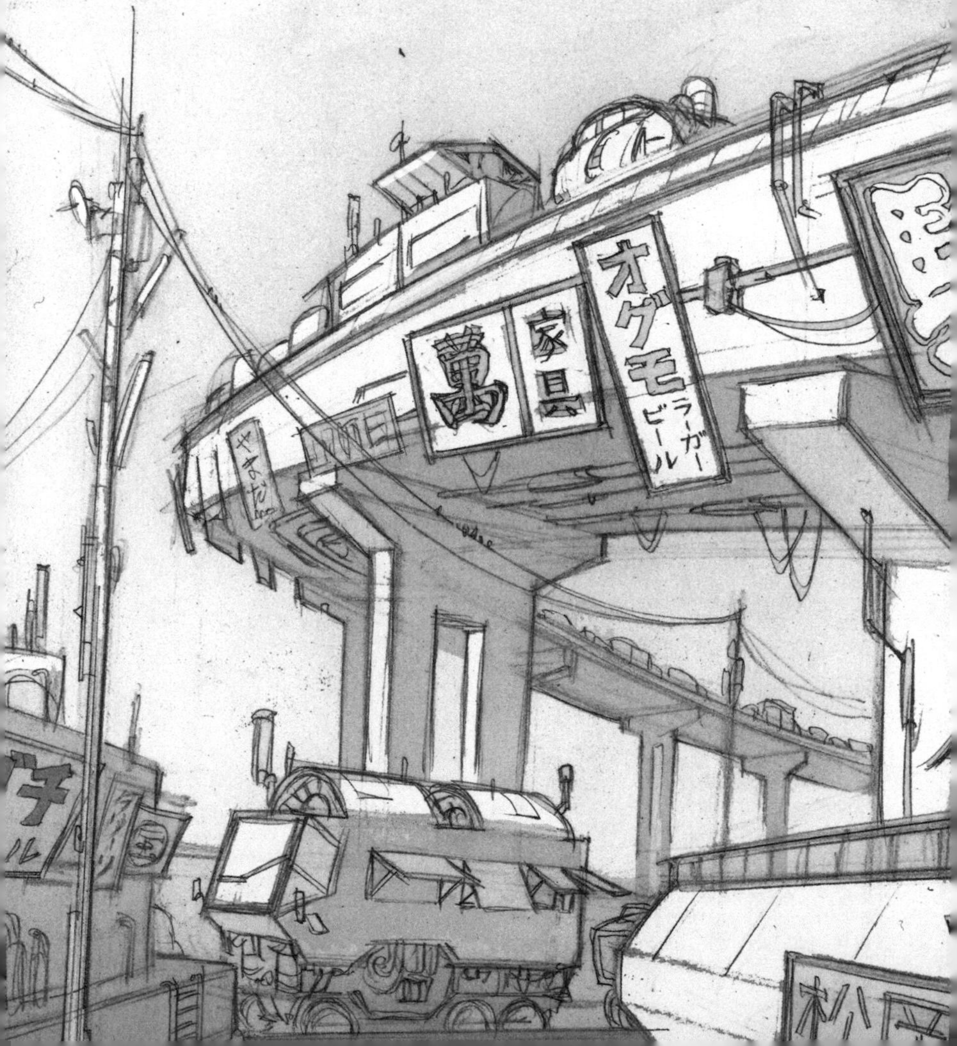

オグモ
ラーガー
ビール
家具
萬
やまだ

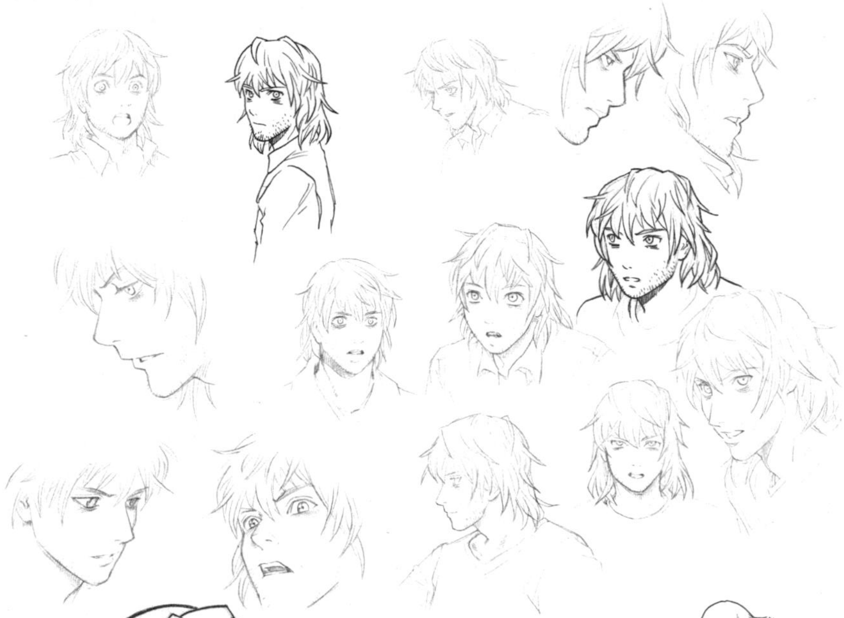

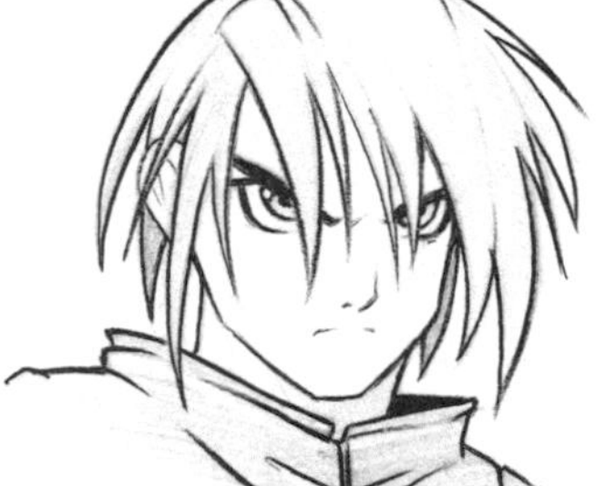

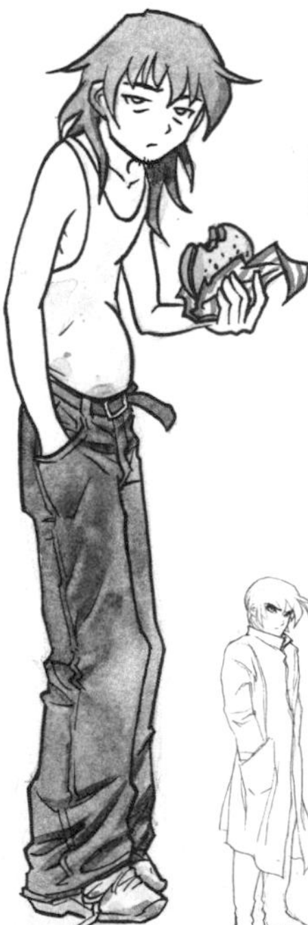

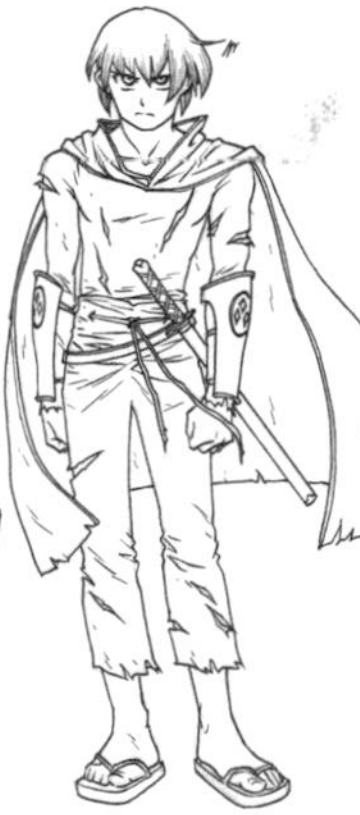

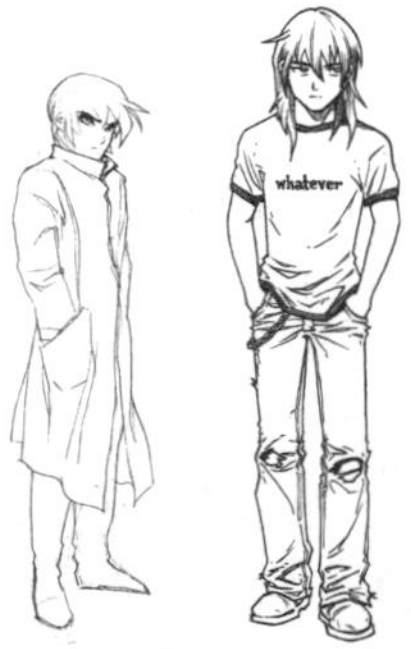
whatever

Brody's character design was developed over a two-year period. At first I saw him as quite cartoony, a look you can see on display here in the hamburger-wielding Brody at right.

As time went on I felt the seriousness of the story would require a more anatomically realistic figure. So I embarked on a series of studies (above) to teach myself how to draw him this way. These studies owe a lot to Takeshi Obata's illustrations of Light Yagami in Death Note*, and even in the final book you can see the debt I owe to him whenever I draw Brody.*

Brody will eventually undergo a radical transformation into a more heroic figure. Here you can see my first attempts at envisioning the "new" Brody that will emerge later in the series.

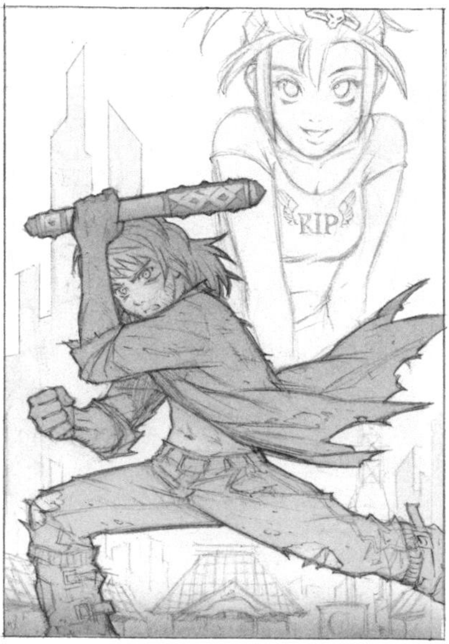
RIP

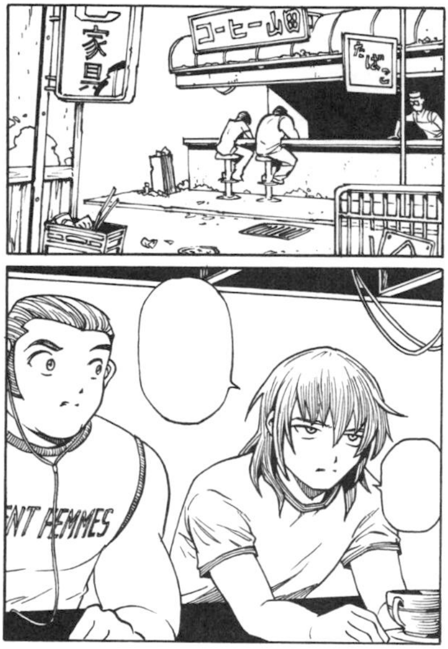
家具
コーヒー山田
たばこ
NT FEMMES

Brody's friend Gabriel was at first going to be a big music geek: note the Violent Femmes T-shirt in the inking test above. I knew Kagemura's decaying temple was going to be a very important location, so I did a detailed concept illustration (below) to help me get a feel for it.

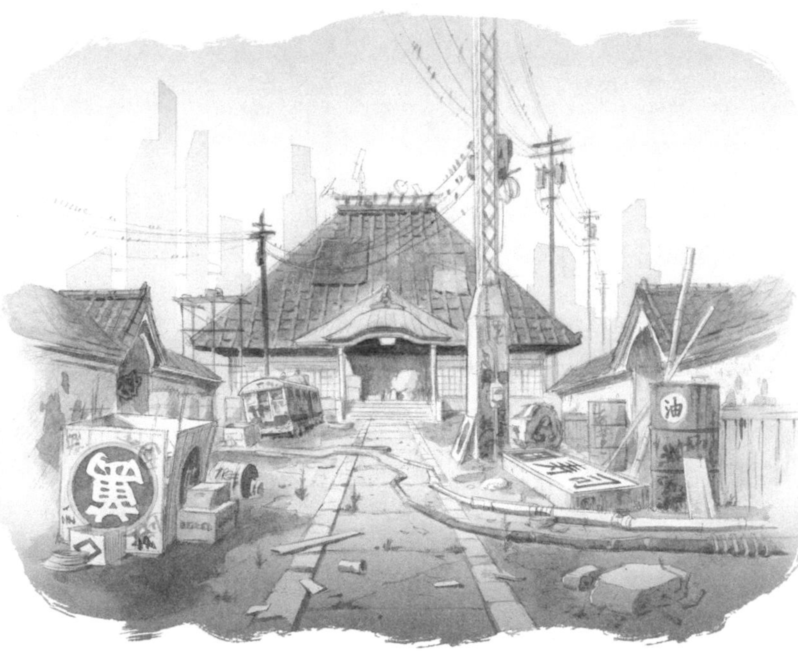
油

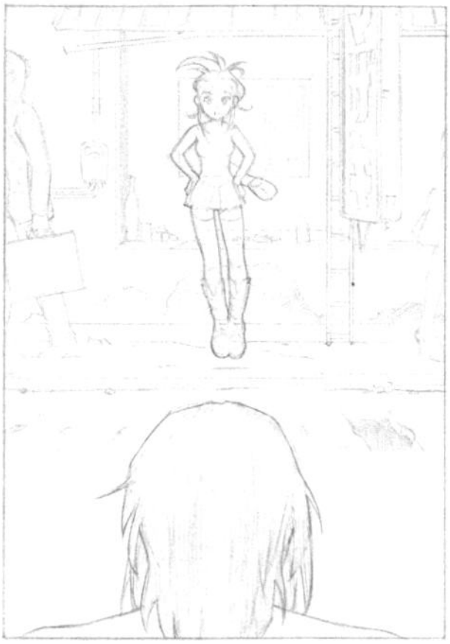

At one point I thought I might have Brody seeing Talia on the very first page of the book as a way of hooking the reader (above). I eventually decided we needed to know Brody first, at least a little, in order to care about the supernatural event he was experiencing.

Like Brody, Talia also started out as quite a cartoony character, and in a very similar way I turned to Takeshi Obata's illustrations (this time looking at Death Note's Misa Amane) for a crash course in combining manga style with more realistic facial proportions.

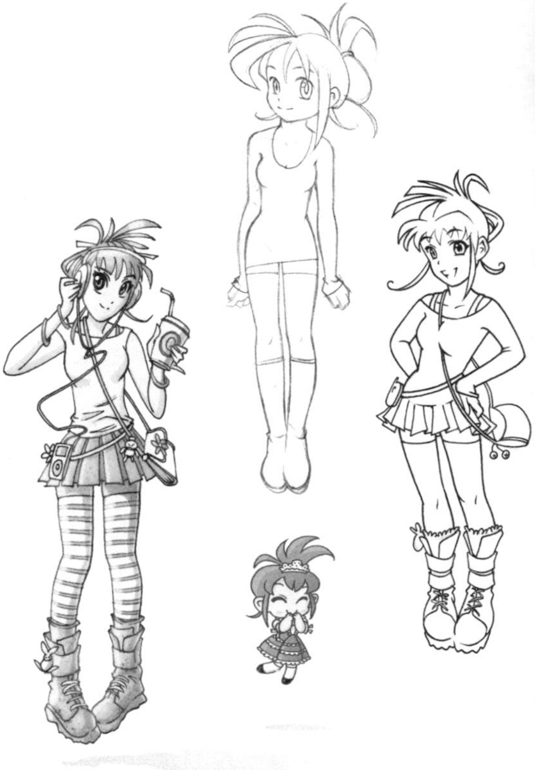

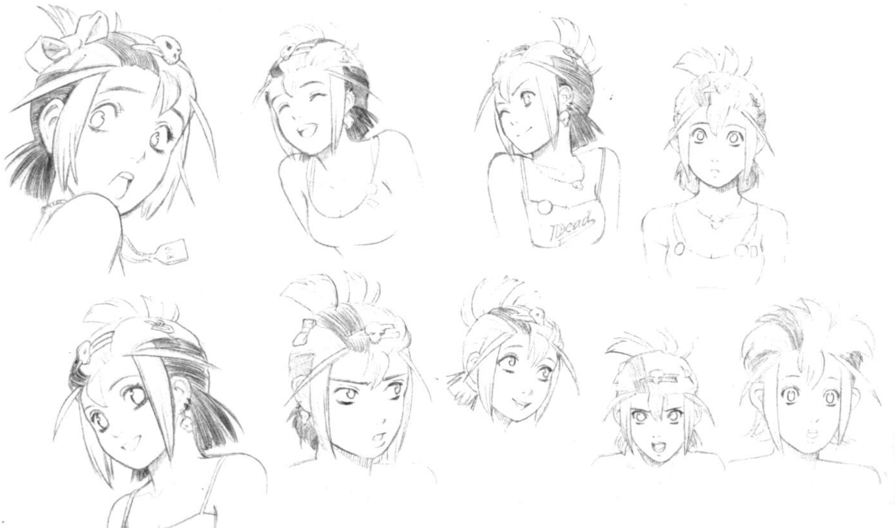
Dead

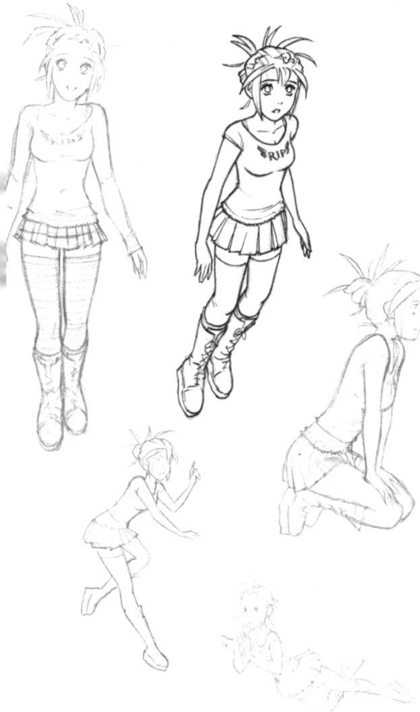
RIP

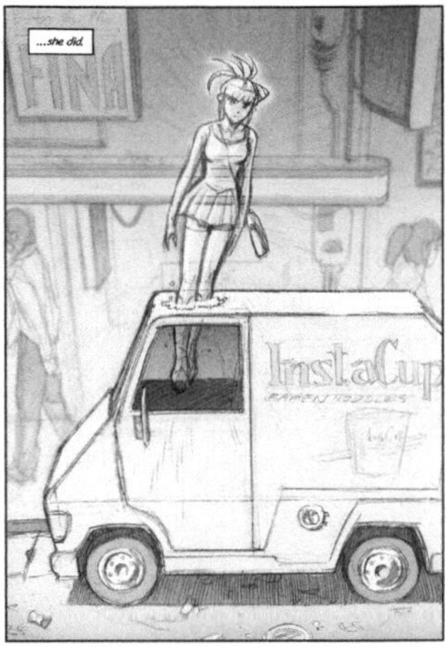
...she did.
InstaCup

The page of Talia rising out of the delivery van was radically redesigned after I decided the first attempt (above) lacked drama. For a time I thought Talia might have dyed streaks in her hair. I also tried out various clothing combinations for her before settling on the RIP T-shirt, which has its origins in the sketch below.

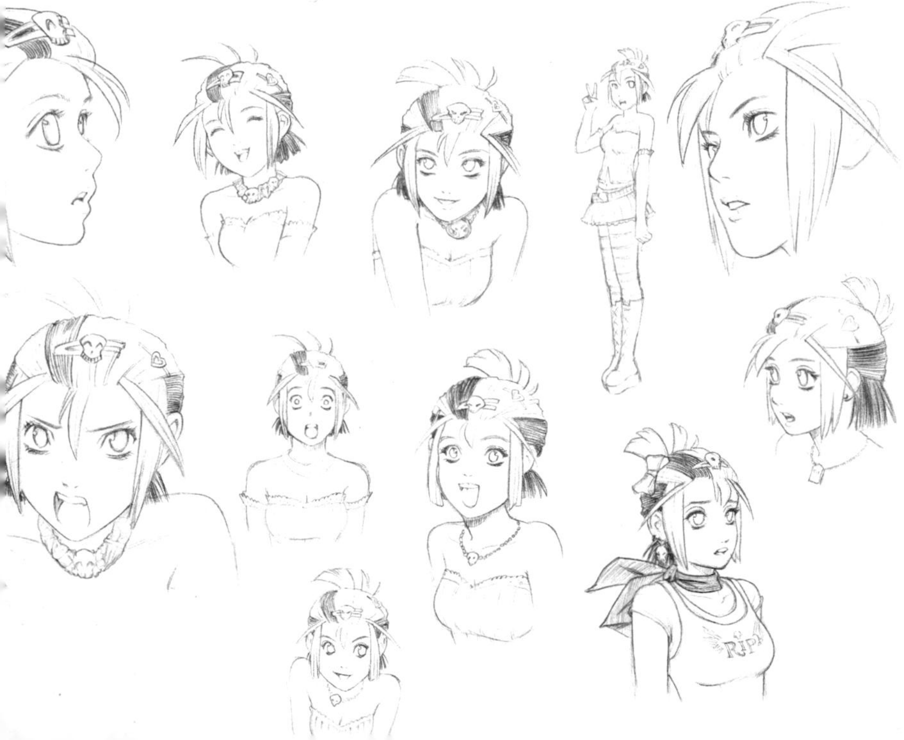
RIP

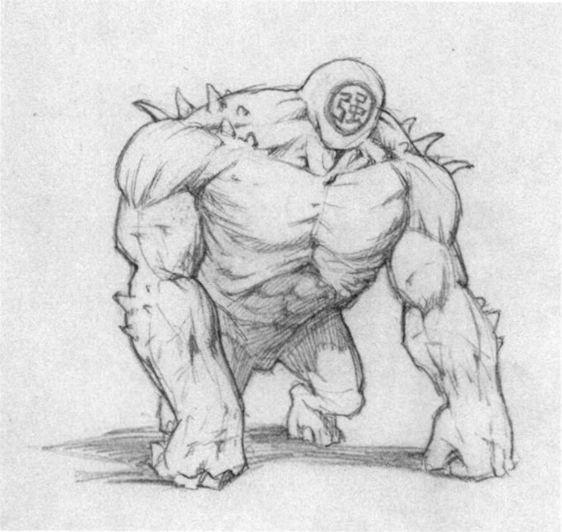

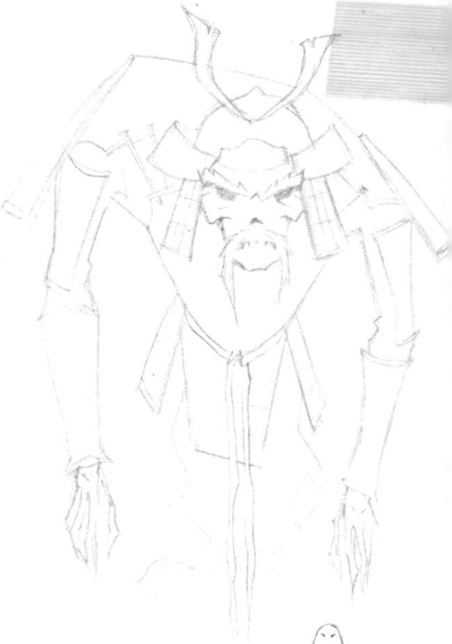

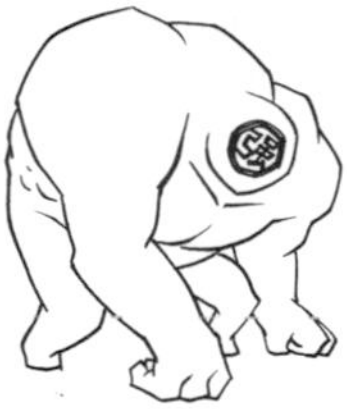

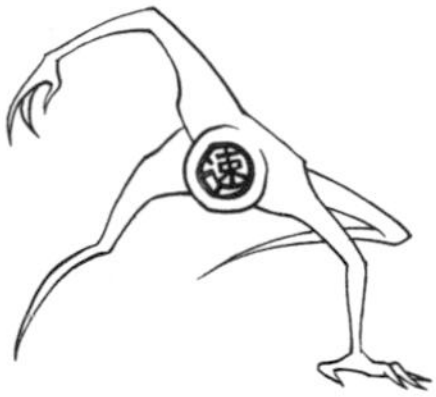

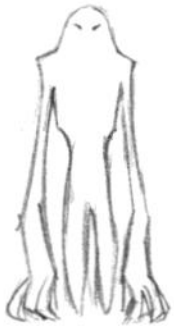

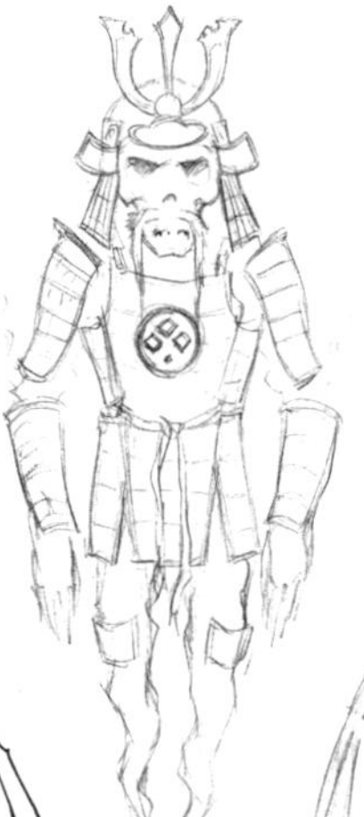

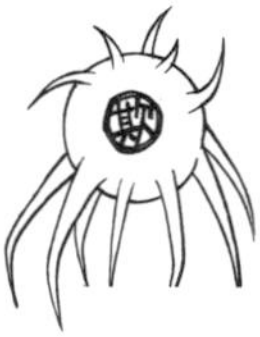

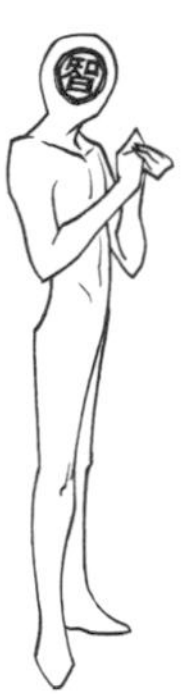

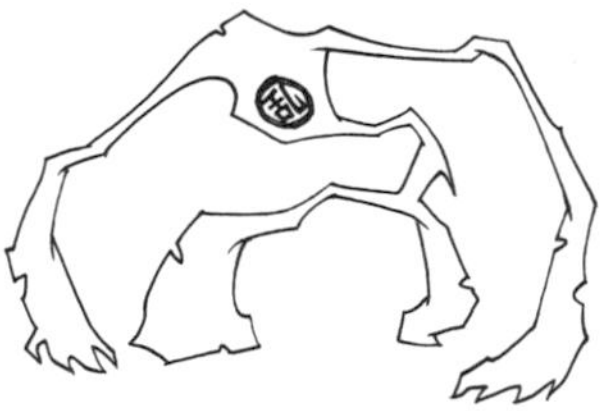

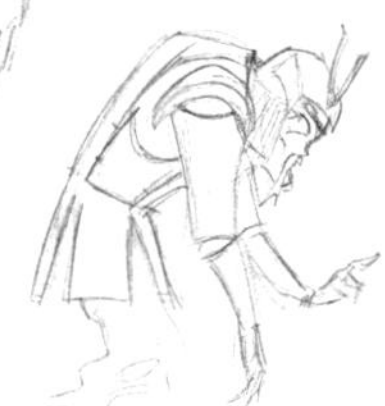

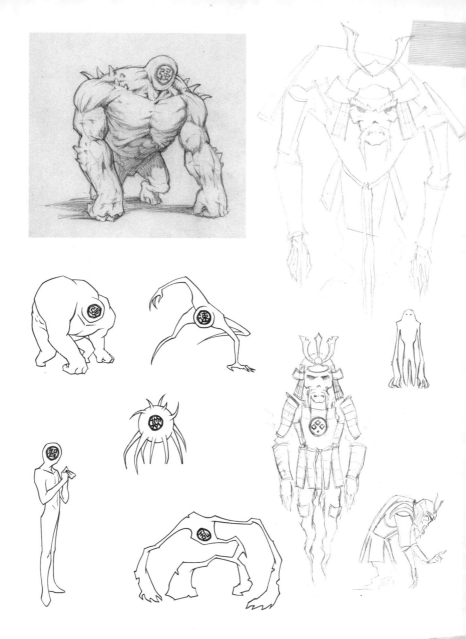

Kagemura has changed a bit since I first began sketching him, but the basic concept was there from the start. His demighost Kyo is just one of five such beings he has at his disposal. I look forward to unveiling the others when the story continues in book 2.

BRODY'S GHOST™